*ideals*

# Christmas Around the World
## COOKBOOK

Ideals Publishing Corp.
Milwaukee, Wisconsin

Introduction

Throughout the world, Christmas is a time of religious observance and traditional feasting. The common denominator of the season everywhere is the lavish preparation of meals to be enjoyed with family and friends.

Quite often the mode of feasting and the dishes served reflect the religious and secular celebrations of a particular people. For instance, the people of Italy, Hungary, Poland, Spain, and Russia observe a religiously inspired meatless Christmas Eve dinner. The next day brings an elaborate Christmas Day feast. The French, after Midnight Mass on Christmas Eve, enjoy a festive supper which includes the log-shaped *Buche de Noel,* or Yule Log. This light cake, filled with custard cream and coated with a chocolate frosting, symbolizes the ancient and secular custom of the lighting of the Yule log.

On Christmas Eve in Poland, the table is covered with a white cloth for good luck and set with extra places for absent family members and a special place for the Christ Child. In a special religious observance, the family partakes of *Oplatki,* small white wafers, which symbolize the Sacred Host.

Because the food and the traditions at Christmastime are as numerous as people on the earth, this cookbook contains only a few of the special dishes of the season. Each chapter presents only one of a country's traditional Christmas or holiday menus. Many of the dishes, because of their popularity, can be prepared in a variety of ways; but the recipes chosen represent what we believe is the most traditional method of preparation.

We wish you pleasure in your holiday preparations and trust that the menus in this book will lend an international flavor to your holidays.

ISBN 0-8249-3008-8  295

Published by Ideals Publishing Corporation
11315 Watertown Plank Road
Milwaukee, Wisconsin 53226
Published simultaneously in Canada.

**Cover recipes**
Oyster Bisque, 4
Roast Prime Rib of Beef, 4
Roast Onions, 4
Creamed Spinach with Croutons, 5


Written by Antonia Manganaro
Photographs by Jerry Koser
Designed by Kevin Walzak


Acknowledgments
Cover and picture, page 7,
photographed at
the Charles Allis Art Museum,
Milwaukee, Wisconsin.

3

# Christmas Day Menu for Six

*England*

Oyster Bisque
Roast Prime Rib of Beef
Roast Onions
Yorkshire Pudding
Creamed Spinach with Croutons
Christmas Trifle
Plum Pudding

## Oyster Bisque

½ cup butter
1 cup minced celery
¼ cup minced shallots
liquid from 1 quart oysters
5 cups milk
1 cup heavy cream

Melt the butter in a heavy kettle. Add the celery and shallots. Cook, stirring, for 10 minutes over moderately low heat until vegetables are soft. Pour in the strained liquid, milk and cream. Bring the mixture to a simmer.

4 egg yolks
1 cup simmering milk mixture
1 quart shucked oysters
salt and pepper to taste
paprika to taste

Beat the egg yolks lightly in a small bowl. Whisk the hot milk mixture into the egg yolks; stir the milk-egg mixture into the kettle. Add the oysters, salt and pepper. Simmer, stirring, until bisque is lightly thickened, and the edges of the oysters have curled. Do not let the bisque come to a boil. Transfer to a heated tureen and sprinkle with the paprika.

## Roast Prime Rib of Beef

1 10-pound beef roast
salt and pepper

Have your butcher trim the short ribs from the roast. Place the meat in a dish and let it come to room temperature. Rub on all sides with salt and pepper. Place the meat on a rack in a shallow roasting pan. Roast in a preheated 450° oven for 25 minutes. Reduce the heat to 325° and roast 2 hours longer for medium-rare. Transfer the roast to a heated platter. Cover loosely and let stand for 15 minutes before carving.

1 cup beef broth
salt and pepper to taste

For the au Jus:
Spoon off any excess fat from the roasting pan. Measure out ½ cup of the beef juices and reserve for the Yorkshire pudding. Pour the beef broth into the roasting pan. Bring to a simmer over moderately high heat, scraping up any brown bits clinging to the bottom and sides of the pan. Season with salt and pepper. Strain the roasting juices into a heated sauceboat and serve with the roast.

## Roast Onions

3 tablespoons butter
10 yellow onions, quartered
salt and pepper to taste

Heat the butter in a large, heavy skillet until it is foaming. Add the onion quarters in quantities that fit easily in the pan. Toss the onions over moderate heat until well coated on all sides. Transfer to a shallow baking dish. Sprinkle the onions with salt and pepper. Bake in a preheated 350° oven for 1 hour and 15 minutes, turning the onion every 20 minutes during roasting.

## Yorkshire Pudding

Sift together the flour and salt in a large mixing bowl. Add the milk, water and eggs. Beat the mixture until smooth. Cover the bowl and let stand at room temperature for 2 hours.

Pour the beef drippings into a shallow 10 x 15-inch baking dish. Place in a preheated 450° oven 10 minutes. Stir the batter again and pour into the baking dish. Bake 15 minutes. Reduce the heat to 350° and bake 20 to 30 minutes, until the pudding is puffed and golden.

3¾ cups all-purpose flour
1 teaspoon salt
1¼ cups milk
¾ cup water
4 eggs

the ½ cup reserved drippings
   from the roasting pan

## Creamed Spinach with Croutons

Wash the spinach in cold water; drain. Drop into a kettle of boiling, salted water. Return the water to a boil. Cook slowly, uncovered, for 5 minutes. Drain the spinach in a colander. Immediately rinse under cold running water for 1 minute. Squeeze the spinach, a handful at a time, to extract as much water as possible. Chop very fine.

3 pounds fresh spinach
boiling, salted water

Heat the butter until bubbling in a saucepan over moderately high heat. Stir in the spinach. Continue stirring for 2 to 3 minutes until all the moisture has evaporated. Season with salt, pepper and nutmeg. Lower the heat to moderate. Sprinkle on the flour and cook, stirring, for 2 minutes.

2 tablespoons butter
the chopped spinach
salt and pepper to taste
pinch nutmeg
1½ tablespoons flour

Remove the pan from the heat. Add the cream by spoonfuls while stirring until ⅔ cup has been added. Return to the heat and bring to a simmer. Cover and cook very slowly for 15 minutes, stirring occasionally and adding the remaining ⅓ cup cream by spoonfuls.

1 cup heavy cream

Remove the spinach from the heat. Stir in the butter. Transfer the creamed spinach to a deep serving dish and mound it decoratively with a spatula. Garnish the spinach with sieved egg yolks and croutons.

1 tablespoon butter
the sieved yolks from
   2 hard-boiled eggs

For the croutons:
Cut decorative shapes out of the bread using a Christmas cookie cutter. Toast the bread shapes under the preheated broiler. Place around the spinach for garnish.

1 or 2 slices of bread

## Christmas Trifle

Butter the bottom and sides of the pans. Line with waxed paper. Butter the paper and dust lightly with the flour. Set the pans aside.

softened butter
11 x 16-inch jelly roll pan
8-inch square cake pan
2 tablespoons flour

Beat the egg yolks, sugar and vanilla with an electric mixer until the mixture is light and ribbons when the beater is lifted.

6 egg yolks
½ cup sugar
1 teaspoon vanilla

Beat the egg whites with the salt until they hold stiff peaks. Fold one-fourth of the egg whites into the yolk mixture. Pour the yolk mixture on top of the remaining egg whites and sprinkle on the flour. Fold the mixture together. Pour into the prepared jelly roll pan and 1-inch

6 egg whites
pinch salt
½ cup flour

deep into the prepared cake pan. Bake in a preheated 350° oven for 15 minutes or until lightly browned. Invert the cake onto a rack or baking sheet to cool. Peel off the waxed paper.

**the cooled cakes**
**8 ounces raspberry jelly**

Split the 11 x 16-inch cake in half crosswise. Spread one half with some of the raspberry jelly. Top with the other half of the cake. Cut the layered cake into triangles.

**1½ quart glass serving bowl**
**12 almond macaroons,**
**crumbled**
**½ cup brandy**

Line the bottom of the bowl with the sandwiched triangles. Line the sides of the bowl with the triangles alternately pointing up, then down, leaving about ⅓ inch between each triangle. Fill the spaces between triangles with the remaining raspberry jelly. Cut the 8-inch square cake into small pieces and sprinkle inside the bowl along with the macaroons. Sprinkle with the brandy.

**12 egg yolks**
**⅓ cup sugar**
**2 cups scalded milk**
**2 cups scalded cream**
**1 tablespoon vanilla**

For the custard:
Beat the egg yolks and sugar in a large bowl until the mixture is light and ribbons when the beater is lifted. Pour on the milk and cream in a stream while beating. Transfer the mixture to a heavy saucepan. Cook over low heat, stirring, until thickened. Do not let it boil. Remove from the heat and stir in the vanilla. Pour the hot custard into a metal bowl. Place the bowl in a larger bowl filled with cracked ice. Stir the custard until cool. Pour the cooled custard on top of the crumbled cake and macaroons, filling the bowl to within ¾ inch of the top. Chill, covered, for at least 6 hours.

**1 cup whipping cream**
**2 tablespoons sugar**
**1 tablespoon brandy**
**red maraschino cherries, split**
**angelica leaves**
**blanched sliced almonds**

Beat the cream with the sugar and brandy until it holds stiff peaks. Place in a pastry bag fitted with a fluted tip and pipe the whipped cream over the edges of the cake sandwiches. Pipe a large rosette in the center of the custard. Decorate the trifle with the cherries and angelica leaves. Sprinkle with the almonds and serve.

## Plum Pudding

**1 cup seedless raisins**
**1 cup dried currants**
**¼ pound mixed candied fruit**
**peel, diced**
**2½ cups beef suet, diced**
**2 cups flour**
**1 cup brown sugar**
**1 teaspoon each ground cloves,**
**cinnamon and nutmeg**
**¼ teaspoon salt**
**grated rind from 1 lemon**
**2 large eggs**
**1 cup light cream**
**¼ cup brandy**

In a deep mixing bowl combine the raisins, currants, candied fruit peel, beef suet, flour, brown sugar, spices, salt and lemon rind. Blend the ingredients thoroughly.

In another bowl beat the eggs with the cream and brandy. Pour over the dried fruit mixture and blend well. Cover the bowl and let stand in a cool place for 12 hours.

Transfer to a large pudding mold. Cover tightly with waxed paper and foil. Place in a deep pan. Add enough boiling water to reach ⅓ the way up the side of the mold. Cover the pan and steam for 4½ hours, adding more water as necessary. When cooked, remove from the water and let stand until cooled. Cover with fresh waxed paper and foil. Refrigerate for 2 weeks for best flavor.

**2 tablespoons heated brandy**
**whipped cream**

To serve the pudding, steam a second time for 2 hours. Turn the pudding onto a heated serving plate. Pour on the hot brandy and light. Serve with whipped cream.

Irish Soda Bread
Consommé with Celery
Roast Turkey
   with Chestnut and Sausage Stuffing
Creamed Brussels Sprouts
Mincemeat Pie

### Irish Soda Bread

3 cups whole wheat flour
1 cup all-purpose flour
2 teaspoons salt
1 teaspoon baking soda
¾ teaspoon baking powder
1½ cups, or more, buttermilk

Combine the flours, salt, baking soda and baking powder in a bowl. Mix thoroughly. Add the buttermilk, working with your hands to make a dough firm enough to hold its shape. Add more buttermilk if necessary. Knead the dough on a lightly floured board for 2 to 3 minutes. The texture should be smooth and velvety. Form into a round loaf. Place on a well-buttered baking sheet. Cut a cross into the top of the loaf with a knife. Bake in a preheated 375° oven for 35 to 40 minutes. The loaf is done when it is browned and has a hollow sound when tapped. Cool on a wire rack.

### Consommé with Celery

4 pounds meaty beef shanks
2 onions, quartered
1 carrot, quartered
3½ quarts water
2 cups water
2 celery ribs
1½ teaspoons salt
4 sprigs parsley
1 bay leaf
⅛ teaspoon thyme

Have your butcher saw the beef shanks into 1-inch pieces. Spread the shanks, onion and carrot in a large baking pan. Brown in a preheated 450° oven for 20 minutes, turning once. Transfer the meat and vegetables to a kettle, adding the 3½ quarts water. Pour the 2 cups water into the baking pan; bring to a boil, scraping up any bits of meat or vegetables clinging to the bottom. Pour the liquid into the kettle. Add the celery, salt, parsley, bay leaf and thyme. Bring to a boil, skimming away any froth that rises to the surface. Simmer gently, uncovered, for 3 hours. Add boiling water, if necessary, to keep the ingredients covered.

1 5- to 7-pound stewing hen, halved
neck, heart and gizzard of hen, chopped

Add the hen, neck, heart and gizzard to the beef stock. Add boiling water to cover. Skim away any froth that rises to the surface. Simmer, uncovered, for 2 to 3 hours or until liquid is reduced to 2 quarts. Remove the hen. Strain the stock and let cool. Chill until the fat solidifies on the surface. Scrape away the fat. Bring the stock to a simmer.

3 tablespoons butter
1½ cups chopped celery ribs and leaves
½ cup chopped leek
½ cup minced celery leaves
salt and pepper to taste

Melt the butter in a kettle. Add the chopped celery and leek. Cover and let the vegetables steam for 20 minutes. Add the beef stock and simmer, uncovered, for 30 minutes. Strain. Salt and pepper to taste. Garnish the consommé with the minced celery leaves.

### Roast Turkey with Chestnut and Sausage Stuffing

1 10- to 12-pound turkey
salt and pepper

Wash the turkey under cold water. Pat dry. Lightly salt and pepper inside and outside of the bird. Set aside.

Ireland

**For the stuffing:**

Set the chestnuts in a pan and cover with cold water. Boil for 1 minute. Remove from heat. Remove 3 chestnuts at a time from the hot water. Peel and remove inner skins. Place the chestnuts in a saucepan. Add the bouillon and water to cover the nuts by 1½ inches. Add the celery, parsley and bay leaf. Simmer, uncovered, for 45 to 60 minutes or until the chestnuts are cooked through. Drain.

1½ pounds fresh chestnuts
1 cup beef bouillon
1 celery rib
2 sprigs parsley
½ bay leaf

Heat the butter in a skillet. Add the onion. Cook for 8 to 10 minutes until soft. Transfer the onion to a mixing bowl. Put the turkey liver in the skillet. Sauté until just browned. Add to the onion. Pour the wine into the skillet. Boil until the wine is reduced to ¼ cup. Add to the onion. Add the pork, veal, pork fat, eggs, salt, thyme, pepper and allspice to the onion. Stir with a wooden spoon until thoroughly blended.

2 tablespoons butter
½ cup chopped onion
the turkey liver, minced
½ cup port or Madeira wine
¾ pound ground pork
¾ pound ground veal
½ pound ground pork fat
2 eggs, beaten
1½ teaspoons salt
½ teaspoon thyme
pinch each pepper and allspice

Stuff the turkey neck and body cavities loosely with alternate layers of the meat mixture and chestnuts. Close the cavities with skewers and lace with kitchen string. Truss the bird securely with kitchen string.

Brush the turkey generously with the butter. Fold the cheesecloth in half crosswise forming a square. Dip the cheesecloth into the remaining melted butter and lay over the turkey breast. Set the turkey on a rack in a shallow roasting pan. Roast in a preheated 325° oven, basting occasionally. A 10- to 12-pound stuffed turkey will take about 4 to 4½ hours to roast. To test for doneness, pierce a thigh with a fork. Juices should run clear yellow.

1 cup butter, melted
8 x 16-inch piece of
   cheesecloth
wire rack
shallow roasting pan

**For the gravy:**

Prepare the gravy while the turkey is roasting. Heat the oil in a large saucepan. Stir in the giblets. Brown on all sides and transfer to a side dish. Put the onion and carrots in the pan. Cover and cook slowly for 5 minutes. Uncover and brown lightly for 5 minutes. Add the browned giblets, wine, chicken stock, bay leaf and thyme. Add water to cover the ingredients by 1 inch. Simmer, partially covered, for 2½ to 3 hours. Strain the stock. Skim the fat from the surface. Blend the cornstarch and wine in a bowl. Stir into the stock. Simmer for 2 to 3 minutes until just thickened. Set aside.

3 tablespoons vegetable oil
the turkey giblets, chopped
1 onion, chopped
2 carrots, chopped
1 cup dry white wine
2 cups chicken stock
1 bay leaf
½ teaspoon thyme
3 tablespoons cornstarch
¼ cup port wine

Transfer the turkey to a heated platter when it is done. Remove the strings and skewers, cover loosely and let stand for 20 to 30 minutes. Scoop the stuffing into a warm dish when ready to serve. Spoon excess fat from the roasting pan. Pour the turkey stock into the roasting pan. Stir over moderately high heat, scraping up the turkey bits from the bottom. Skim any fat from the surface of the gravy. Pour into a warm sauceboat and serve with the turkey and stuffing.

the turkey stock

## Creamed Brussels Sprouts

Cut a cross in the base of each sprout. Drop into boiling salted water. Boil slowly, uncovered, for 6 to 8 minutes. Drain. Lay the sprouts in one layer on a towel to cool.

1½ quarts Brussels sprouts

Butter a shallow baking dish. Arrange the sprouts in two layers in the dish. Sprinkle lightly with salt, pepper and melted butter. Set over moderate heat, cover and cook until the sprouts begin to sizzle. Transfer to a preheated 350° oven for 10 minutes.

the blanched sprouts
salt and pepper
2 tablespoons butter, melted

Bring the cream to a boil. Pour boiling cream into the dish and continue to bake for 10 minutes more. Dot the sprouts with butter and serve.

¾ cup heavy cream
2 tablespoons butter

## Mincemeat Pie

For the filling:
Core the apple but do not peel. Mince the apple, raisins, currants, sultana raisins, candied fruit peel and almonds. Combine in a large mixing bowl.

1 large apple
2 cups raisins
2 cups currants
1 cup sultana raisins
½ cup candied fruit peel
½ cup almonds

Combine the orange and lemon rind, sugar, salt, cinnamon, allspice and cloves in a small bowl. Stir with a fork to blend thoroughly. Sprinkle in the minced fruit and almonds. Blend with a fork.

grated rind from 1 orange
grated rind from 1 lemon
1 cup sugar
¼ teaspoon each salt, ground cloves, cinnamon and allspice

Combine the orange juice, lemon juice and whiskey in a cup. Pour over the minced fruit mixture. Pour the butter over the ingredients and blend. Pour the filling into a glass jar, cover tightly and refrigerate overnight.

juice of 1 orange
juice of 1 lemon
¼ cup Irish whiskey
½ cup butter, melted

For the pastry crust:
Combine the flour, salt, and sugar in a bowl. Cut in the butter and shortening. Mix with a pastry blender until the mixture resembles coarse meal. Add the water to the dough, a little at a time, while gathering the dough into a ball. Wrap with waxed paper and refrigerate for 2 hours.

2 cups all-purpose flour
½ teaspoon salt
¼ teaspoon sugar
¼ pound chilled butter, cut into ½-inch pieces
3 tablespoons chilled shortening
3 tablespoons, or more, cold water

Assembling the pie:
Roll out the dough ⅛ inch thick on a lightly floured surface and line a 9-inch pie pan allowing a 1-inch overhang. Cover and chill.

Roll the remaining dough into a rectangle ¼ inch thick and 12 inches long. Cut the dough into ½-inch wide strips. Fill the shell with the mincemeat. Lay the strips of dough over the pie in a lattice pattern. Turn up the edges and crimp decoratively. Bake in a preheated 425° oven for 20 minutes. Reduce heat to 350° and bake for 30 minutes until golden.

*Christmas Punch
Cheese Pastries
Pea Soup with Champagne
Roast Goose
Apple Halves Stuffed with Prunes
Sugar=Browned Potatoes
Rice and Almond Pudding
Vanilla Wreaths*

### Christmas Punch

rind of ½ lemon
2¼ pints dry red wine
1 cinnamon stick
3 cloves
8 cardamom seeds
½ cup sugar
½ cup chopped almonds
½ cup seedless raisins
1 cup Cognac

Shave the outermost yellow peel from the lemon with a vegetable peeler. Cut the peel into ⅛-inch strips. Combine the sliced lemon rind, red wine, cinnamon stick, cloves, cardamom seeds, sugar, almonds and raisins in a large saucepan. Stir over low heat until the sugar is dissolved. Just before it reaches a boil, transfer to a serving bowl. Add the Cognac just before serving. Light it with a match and ladle into punch cups.

### Cheese Pastries

⅔ cup softened butter
1⅔ cups grated Gruyére cheese
2 cups all-purpose flour
1½ teaspoons salt
1 teaspoon paprika
½ teaspoon baking powder
½ cup heavy cream

Blend the butter and cheese in a bowl. Combine the flour, salt, paprika and baking powder in another bowl. Blend well with a fork. Add the flour mixture and heavy cream alternately to the butter and cheese mixture. Blend until a soft dough forms. Form into a ball. Wrap in waxed paper; chill for 1 hour.

1 egg yolk
2 tablespoons water
sliced blanched almonds
poppy seed

Roll out the dough ⅛-inch thick on a lightly floured work surface. Cut with decorative Christmas cookie cutters. Put the cut-out shapes on a lightly buttered baking sheet. Combine the egg yolk and water in a small bowl; brush on the pastries. Sprinkle half the pastries with the almonds. Sprinkle the other half with the poppy seed. Bake the pastries in a preheated 375° oven for 12 minutes until puffed and golden. Serve warm with the soup course.

### Pea Soup with Champagne

3 cups shelled fresh peas or
20 ounces frozen peas
1 carrot
1 medium onion, quartered
¾-ounce slab bacon rind
1 small bay leaf
pinch each sage, chervil
and thyme

Combine the peas, carrot, onion, bacon rind, bay leaf, sage, chervil and thyme in a saucepan. Cover with cold water. Bring to a boil. Reduce heat and simmer, covered, for 15 minutes, until the peas are soft. Remove from heat. Discard the carrot, onion, bacon rind and bay leaf. Press the peas and their liquid through a sieve into a bowl.

Return the puree to the pan. Stir in the chicken stock, sherry, lemon juice, salt and pepper to taste. Bring to a boil, stirring.

3 cups chicken bouillon
⅓ cup dry sherry
lemon juice
salt and pepper

Beat the cream until it forms stiff peaks. Fold into the pea mixture. Pour in the champagne. Ladle the soup into heated bowls and serve.

¾ cup heavy cream
1 split bottle of champagne, at room temperature

## Roast Goose Stuffed with Apples and Prunes

In a small bowl, soak the prunes in hot water to cover for 5 minutes. Pit and chop the prunes.

2 cups dried prunes
hot water

Wash the goose under cold running water; pat dry with a towel. Rub the bird inside and out with the lemon. Lightly salt and pepper the inside and stuff the cavity with the apples, prunes and onion quarters. Close the opening of the bird with skewers and lace with kitchen string. With a skewer, close the neck opening. Truss the bird securely with kitchen string. With a fork, prick the skin around the thighs, back and lower breast so the fat will drain during roasting. Place the goose, breast side up, in the roasting pan and set in the middle of a preheated 425° oven for 15 minutes, to brown lightly. Reduce oven to 350° and turn the goose on one side. Remove fat occasionally with a bulb baster during roasting. Baste every 15 to 20 minutes with boiling water to help dissolve the fat. After 1 hour, turn the goose on the other side. An 8-pound stuffed goose will take about 2 hours and 20 minutes; a 10-pound stuffed bird will take about 25 minutes longer. Fifteen minutes before the end of the estimated roasting time, salt the goose and turn breast side up. To test whether the bird is done, pierce the thigh with a small knife. If the juice is rosy-colored, roast another 5 to 10 minutes, or until the juice runs clear yellow. When done, discard trussing string and skewers. Scoop out the apples, prunes and onions; discard. (They will have accumulated fat from the goose, but they will have imparted their flavor to the meat.) Set bird on a heated platter, covered, for 15 minutes before carving.

1 8- to 10-pound young goose
½ lemon
salt and pepper
2 cups peeled, cored and chopped apples
the chopped prunes
1 large onion, peeled and quartered
skewers
kitchen string

## Apple Halves Stuffed with Prunes

Combine the wine and sugar in a small saucepan. Bring to a simmer; stir to dissolve the sugar. Add the prunes and simmer, very gently, for 20 minutes or until prunes are just tender. Remove from heat and cool. Cover and refrigerate for 6 hours.

⅔ cup port wine
2 teaspoons sugar
12 medium prunes

Core and peel the apples; cut them in half, lengthwise. In a 2- to 3-quart saucepan, combine the sugar and water and boil for 2 to 3 minutes. Lower the heat and add 6 apple halves. Simmer for 10 minutes until just tender. Remove the apples from the saucepan and keep warm. Poach the remaining 6 apple halves.

6 large baking apples
1 cup sugar
1 quart cold water

Drain the prunes and place 1 prune in each apple half. These may be prepared in advance and covered with plastic wrap. Refrigerate until 10 minutes before serving time. Preheat oven to 400°. Uncover prune-filled apples and place on a lightly buttered cookie sheet. Bake 10 minutes. Surround the goose with the stuffed apples.

## Sugar-Browned Potatoes

Drop the potatoes into the boiling water and cook 15 to 20 minutes or until tender. Drain off the hot water. Cover the potatoes with cold water and let them set until cool enough to handle, but still warm. Peel the potatoes.

24 small new potatoes
2½ quarts boiling water

Melt the sugar in a heavy skillet over low heat for 3 to 5 minutes. Stir constantly with a wooden spoon. The sugar will turn color very rapidly and will burn easily. The sugar should turn a light brown. Stir in the melted butter and blend until smooth. Add as many potatoes as can easily fit into one layer. Shake the pan constantly to coat the potatoes. Remove the potatoes as they are coated and repeat the same process until all the potatoes are coated.

½ cup sugar
½ cup butter, melted

## Rice and Almond Pudding

Bring the milk to a boil in a heavy saucepan. Add the rice and sugar. Stir to blend. Lower the heat and simmer gently, uncovered, for 25 minutes or until the rice is tender. To test the rice, rub a grain between your thumb and forefinger. If there is no hard kernel in the center, the rice is done. Remove from the heat and cool.

3¾ cups milk
1 cup long grain white rice
⅓ cup sugar
½ cup blanched almonds, chopped
½ cup sweet sherry
1 teaspoon vanilla
¼ teaspoon grated orange rind
pinch nutmeg

When the rice is cool stir in the chopped almonds, sherry, vanilla, grated orange rind and nutmeg.

## Vanilla Wreaths

Beat the cream until it holds a peak in a chilled bowl. Fold into the rice mixture. Pour the pudding into a large serving bowl or divide among serving glasses. Chill well before serving.

1 cup heavy cream

### Vanilla Wreaths

Sift together the flour, sugar, baking powder and salt in a large mixing bowl. Cut the butter into ½-inch pieces and distribute over the flour mixture. Blend the mixture with a pastry blender until it resembles coarse meal. Sprinkle the ground almonds and vanilla over the mixture. Continue to blend until a dough forms. Wrap in waxed paper and chill for 30 minutes.

1¼ cups all-purpose flour
¾ cup sugar
⅛ teaspoon baking powder
pinch salt
½ cup plus 2 tablespoons chilled butter
⅓ cup blanched almonds, ground
½ teaspoon vanilla

Fill a metal cookie press fitted with a ½-inch star plate with the dough. Press 2-inch strips ½ inch apart onto a lightly greased baking sheet. Form each strip into a round, pressing the ends together. Chill the unbaked cookies 15 minutes. Bake in a preheated 375° oven for 8 minutes or until golden. Transfer the cookies to racks and let them cool. Makes about 60 cookies.

Roast Goose, Apple Halves
Stuffed with Prunes, Christmas Punch

## Christmas Day Menu for Six

*Oysters on the Half Shell*
*Paté with Pistachios*
*Shrimp Soup with Curry*
*Chicken Bonne Femme*
*Buche de Noel*

### Oysters on the Half Shell

36 fresh oysters
rock salt
lemon wedges

Scrub the shells under cold water. Force a shucking knife between the shell at the thin end and cut the abductor muscle. Remove the top shell with a twisting motion. Cover 6 serving plates with the rock salt. Arrange 6 oysters on each. Garnish with lemon.

### Paté with Pistachios

1 pound diced pork
1 pound diced veal
1 cup diced pork fat
1 small chicken breast, diced
3 chicken livers

Place the uncooked pork, veal, pork fat, chicken breast and chicken livers in a food processor and grind together. Or put each ingredient through a meat grinder and blend together in a large bowl.

3 tablespoons butter
¾ cup chopped onion
4 cloves garlic, minced

Heat the butter until foaming in a heavy skillet. Add the onion and garlic. Sauté 3 minutes until soft. Add to the meat mixture.

½ cup Madeira or dry sherry
¼ cup Cognac

Pour the Madeira and Cognac into the skillet. Boil until reduced to ⅓ cup. Add to the meat mixture.

3 eggs, lightly beaten
½ cup pistachio nuts
1½ teaspoons salt
½ teaspoon ground pepper
½ bay leaf, crumbled
pinch each ground cloves, sage, ginger, nutmeg, mace, cinnamon, paprika, thyme, basil, marjoram, oregano
an 8-cup terrine
4 or 5 sheets fresh pork fat, cut ⅛ inch thick

Add the eggs, pistachio nuts, salt and pepper to the meat mixture. Add a pinch each of herbs and spices. Stir to blend ingredients thoroughly.

Line an 8-cup terrine with the fat; allow the fat to hang over the sides. Fill with the meat mixture, pressing firmly. Fold fat over the meat to enclose. Wrap the terrine in foil. Place in a baking pan filled with boiling water. Bake 1½ hours in a preheated 350° oven. Remove the terrine from the water. Set on a wire rack. Place a weight on top and let stand 2 hours. Refrigerate overnight.

### Shrimp Soup with Curry

1 pound fish trimmings
2 cups cold water
1½ cups clam juice
1 cup dry white wine
1 onion, sliced
1 teaspoon lemon juice
5 parsley stems

Place the fish trimmings in a large kettle. Add the water, clam juice, white wine, sliced onion, lemon juice and parsley stems. Bring slowly to a simmer. Skim off any fat that rises to the surface. Simmer gently, uncovered, for 30 minutes. Strain through a sieve. Return the fish stock to the saucepan and simmer slowly until ready to use.

3 tablespoons butter
½ cup chopped onion
2 garlic cloves, minced
3 tablespoons flour
1 tablespoon curry powder

Heat the butter in a heavy skillet. Sauté the onion and garlic 5 minutes. Add the flour and curry powder. Cook, stirring constantly, 2 minutes. Remove from the heat. Whisk in the simmering fish stock. Beat until smooth. Return to the heat. Simmer for 5 minutes.

Drain the tomatoes, reserving liquid. Chop and add to the soup. Add tomato liquid, carrots, potato and allspice. Bring to a boil. Reduce heat and simmer, uncovered, for 12 to 15 minutes. Potatoes should be just tender.

8-ounces pear-shaped tomatoes
2 carrots, chopped
1 potato, peeled and diced
pinch allspice

Cut the fish into 2 x ½-inch strips. Add to the soup along with the shrimp. Simmer 3 minutes. Stir in the cream. Add salt and pepper to taste. Stir until heated through. Do not allow to boil. Garnish the soup with lemon slices and fresh minced parsley.

1 pound fish fillets
12 large shrimp, halved
½ cup heavy cream
salt and pepper to taste
lemon slices
fresh parsley, minced

## Chicken Bonne Femme

Rinse the chickens under cold running water. Pat dry inside and out with a towel. Salt the outside and inside of the birds lightly. Set aside.

2 2½- to 3-pound frying
  chickens
salt

Heat the butter until foaming in a large, heavy-bottomed skillet. Add the onion and garlic. Sauté for 2 minutes.

4 tablespoons butter
1 large onion, finely chopped
2 cloves garlic, minced

Cut the potatoes, carrots and zucchini into ¼-inch cubes and add to the skillet. Sauté 2 minutes. Stir in the parsley, salt and pepper.

2 medium potatoes, peeled
3 carrots, peeled
2 medium zucchini
½ cup minced fresh parsley
salt and pepper to taste

Spoon the stuffing into the neck and body cavities of the birds. Close the cavities with skewers. With kitchen string, truss the birds so they hold their shape while roasting. Place breast side up in a shallow roasting pan. Spread 1 tablespoon of the butter over each chicken. Set in a preheated 425° oven 15 minutes to brown.

2 tablespoons softened butter
4 strips of bacon
1 cup dry white wine

Remove chickens from the oven and lay 2 strips of bacon over each. Pour the wine into the pan. Reduce heat to 350° and roast, uncovered, 1¼ hours, basting every 20 minutes. The chickens are done when juices are clear yellow when the thigh is pierced with a fork. Remove to a heated platter. Skim the fat from the pan. Reserve the pan juices.

For the sauce:
Melt the butter in a saucepan. Stir in the flour. Cook, stirring constantly, 3 minutes. Stir in the pan juices with a wire whisk. Heat to a simmer. Whisk in cream. Cook, stirring, until the mixture thickens. Simmer for 1 minute.

2 tablespoons butter
1½ tablespoons flour
the pan juices
1 cup heavy cream

Whisk a small amount of the sauce at a time into egg yolks until ¼ cup has been added. Whisk the egg yolks back into the sauce. Stir over low heat 2 to 3 minutes. Remove from heat. Add salt and white pepper to taste.

2 egg yolks
salt and white pepper

To serve the chicken:
Remove the stuffing from the birds. Mound around the chickens on the platter. Pour some sauce over the birds. Serve the remaining sauce in a sauceboat.

## Buche de Noel (Yule Log Cake)

Place the eggs, egg yolk, sugar and vanilla in a mixing bowl. Place the bowl over a pan of simmering water for a few seconds. Remove from the heat and beat on high speed for 5 to 6 minutes. Sift on the flour and fold in with a rubber spatula. Then pour on the butter in a stream and fold into the batter.

5 large eggs
1 egg yolk
¾ cup sugar
½ teaspoon vanilla
¾ cup all-purpose flour
3 tablespoons melted butter

17

| | |
|---|---|
| **12 by 16-inch jelly roll pan**<br>**waxed paper**<br>**butter**<br>**flour** | Lightly butter the pan and line with a sheet of waxed paper. Butter the waxed paper and dust lightly with the flour. Pour the batter into the pan, spreading it evenly out to the sides. Bake in a preheated 325° oven for 12 minutes. Let the cake set for 5 minutes before unmolding. Lay a piece of waxed paper on the table; turn the cake out on the paper. Remove the waxed paper which covered the bottom of the cake, then cover the cake loosely with it. Let the cake cool to lukewarm. Starting at one of the long sides, roll the cake between the two sheets of waxed paper. Refrigerate until ready to use. |
| **3 egg yolks**<br>**⅓ cup sugar**<br>**½ teaspoon vanilla extract**<br>**¼ cup flour**<br>**1 cup boiling milk**<br>**½ cup heavy cream** | Place the egg yolks, sugar and vanilla in a bowl. Beat until light and mixture ribbons when the beater is lifted. Add the flour and blend together. Add the milk in a stream, stirring with a wire whisk. Transfer the mixture to a saucepan set over moderate heat; stir constantly until the sauce reaches a boil. Reduce heat and cook, stirring, for 2 to 3 minutes longer. Remove from the heat. Cover and cool to room temperature. Whip the cream until it holds stiff peaks. Fold the whipped cream into the custard. Set aside. |
| **3 ounces semisweet chocolate**<br>**2 ounces bittersweet chocolate** | Place the chocolate in a small bowl. Cover and set in a pan of barely simmering water until melted. |
| **⅓ cup sugar**<br>**¼ cup water** | Combine the sugar and water in a saucepan. Boil until the syrup reaches the softball stage (236° to 238° on a candy thermometer). |
| **3 egg yolks**<br>**the sugar syrup**<br>**½ pound unsalted butter,**<br>**softened**<br>**the melted chocolate** | Place the egg yolks in a mixing bowl and begin beating with an electric mixer. Pour the hot sugar syrup over the yolks a few drops at a time while beating at medium speed. Increase speed to high and beat for 5 minutes, until mixture is thick and pale yellow. Reduce speed to low and add the butter, a little at a time. Beat until the mixture is smooth. Place ¼ cup of the buttercream in a small bowl; set aside. Add the melted chocolate to the remaining buttercream and beat until smooth. Set aside. |
| **the cake roll**<br>**the custard-cream** | Unroll the cake. Remove the waxed paper on top. Spread the custard-cream over the cake. Roll the cake up to form a log, removing the waxed paper. Cut a 2-inch diagonal piece from both ends of the cake. Transfer the cake to a platter. Arrange the pieces against the sides of the cake to form branch stumps. |
| **the chocolate buttercream**<br>**the ¼ cup reserved buttercream**<br>**glacéed cherries**<br>**candied angelica or holly** | Using a spatula, spread the chocolate buttercream on the log, reserving ¼ cup for piping. Spread the reserved buttercream over both ends and on tops of the stumps. Pull the tines of a fork down the full length of the cake roll to simulate bark. Fill a pastry bag with the ¼ cup chocolate buttercream. Pipe rings around both ends of the cake and on the ends of the stumps to simulate wood. Decorate the cake with glacéed cherries and candied angelica, cut to look like holly leaves. |

Buche de Noel (Yule Log Cake)

*Christmas Day
Menu for Six*

*Potato and Cucumber Soup
Knockwurst Salad
Red Cabbage
Spaetzle    Carrots in Beer
Sauerbraten with Gingersnap Gravy
Pumpernickel Pudding    Filbert Balls*

## Potato and Cucumber Soup

2 medium cucumbers, peeled

6 boiling potatoes, peeled and quartered
5 cups chicken bouillon

2 tablespoons butter
1 small onion, minced
the chicken and potato stock
2 cups heavy cream
salt and pepper to taste
2 teaspoons dried dillweed

Slice the cucumbers lengthwise. Scoop out the seeds with a small spoon. Dice and set aside.

Combine the potatoes and bouillon in a kettle. Simmer, partially covered, and cook until the potatoes are tender. Press the stock and potatoes through a sieve into a bowl.

Melt the butter in a kettle. Add the onion and sauté for 5 minutes. Add the chicken and potato stock. Stir in the cream, salt, pepper and cucumbers.

Simmer 6 to 8 minutes until the cucumber is tender. Stir in the dillweed and serve.

## Knockwurst Salad

¾ pound knockwurst, cooked
6 tablespoons chopped pickles
½ cup chopped onion

3 tablespoons vegetable oil
3 tablespoons vinegar
1 tablespoon lemon juice
2 tablespoons capers
1½ teaspoons Dijon mustard
½ teaspoon sugar
½ teaspoon salt
pinch paprika
pinch pepper
2 tablespoons chopped parsley

Cool the knockwurst and cut into ½-inch cubes. Combine the knockwurst, pickles and onion in a mixing bowl. Cover and refrigerate for 1 hour.

Combine the vegetable oil, vinegar, lemon juice, capers, mustard, sugar, salt, paprika and pepper in a glass jar. Cover the jar and shake well. Refrigerate for an hour and let set at room temperature for 15 minutes before serving.

Arrange the knockwurst mixture in a shallow salad bowl. Shake the dressing again before pouring onto salad. Garnish with chopped fresh parsley.

## Red Cabbage

1 medium head red cabbage
2 tablespoons vegetable oil
1 cup sliced onion
2 tablespoons vinegar
salt to taste
2 teaspoons sugar
2 tart red cooking apples, peeled, cored and sliced
3 slices bacon
½ cup red wine
½ cup beef broth

Remove the outer leaves from the cabbage and discard. Cut cabbage into quarters and cut out core. Shred cabbage. Heat oil in a large skillet and sauté onion for 3 minutes. Add cabbage and immediately pour vinegar over cabbage to prevent it from losing color. Sprinkle with salt and sugar, tossing to coat cabbage.

Cut the bacon into ½-inch pieces. Add apples and bacon. Pour in red wine and beef broth. Cover and simmer slowly for 45 to 60 minutes until cabbage is just tender but not soft.

## Spaetzle

Combine flour, salt and nutmeg in mixing bowl. Make a well in the center and add the eggs and ¼ cup of the water. Beat until a stiff dough forms. Add water, a little at a time, until dough is firm and comes away from the sides of the bowl easily. Knead until smooth. Let stand in the bowl 30 minutes.

3 cups sifted all-purpose flour
1 teaspoon salt
pinch nutmeg
4 eggs, beaten
½ cup, or more, water

Place the dough in the colander, set over a kettle holding the boiling water. Press dough through the colander. Cook about 5 minutes or until noodles rise to the surface. Remove promptly with a slotted spoon and drain on a towel. Brown noodles in melted butter over low heat. Serve immediately.

colander with ¼-inch holes
2½ quarts boiling salted water
3 tablespoons butter

## Carrots in Beer

Peel the carrots. Cut into long diagonal slices. Heat the butter in a heavy saucepan. Add the carrots, stirring until they are coated with butter. Sprinkle in the sugar and salt. Pour in the beer. Lower the heat and simmer, uncovered, until the carrots are tender. Serve immediately.

8 large carrots
2 tablespoons butter
2 teaspoons sugar
½ teaspoon salt
1½ cups dark beer or lager

## Sauerbraten

Place meat in a large glass bowl. Rub the meat with the salt and pepper. Cover and let come to room temperature. Bring water, vinegar, wine, onion, cloves and bay leaves to a boil in a saucepan. Simmer for 10 minutes. Cool marinade to room temperature. Pour over beef and refrigerate for 2 to 3 days turning meat several times a day.

1 4-pound beef rump roast
1 teaspoon each salt and pepper
2 cups water
1 cup red wine vinegar
1 cup dry red wine
2 cups sliced onion
8 cloves
2 bay leaves

Heat the vegetable oil in a Dutch oven or ovenproof casserole. Add the meat and brown on all sides. Add the tomato, carrots, celery and marinade liquid. Cover and simmer gently for 1½ to 2 hours. Or bring to a simmer on top of the stove, cover and bake in a preheated 325° oven for 1½ to 2 hours.

2 tablespoons vegetable oil
1 medium tomato, peeled, seeded and chopped
1 cup diced carrots
1 cup diced celery

When the meat has finished cooking, remove it from the marinade. Cover the meat and keep warm while preparing the gravy. Remove cloves and bay leaves from marinade. Blend together flour, crushed gingersnaps, sugar and the ¼ cup marinade in a small bowl to make a thick paste. Add to the remaining marinade in the Dutch oven and cook, stirring, until thickened. Spoon some of the gravy over meat. Serve remaining gravy in a sauceboat.

2 tablespoons flour
¼ cup crushed gingersnaps
2 teaspoons sugar
¼ cup marinade

## Pumpernickel Pudding

Butter the mold and coat it well with the bread crumbs. Set aside.

8-cup pudding mold
softened butter
dry bread crumbs

Soak the raisins in the orange liqueur for 30 minutes in a small bowl.

⅓ cup golden raisins
⅓ cup orange liqueur

| | |
|---|---|
| 3 cups fine, pumpernickel bread crumbs<br>1 cup brown sugar<br>⅔ cup ground almonds<br>⅔ cup ground vanilla wafers<br>½ cup plus 3 tablespoons melted butter<br>1 teaspoon grated orange rind<br>1 teaspoon grated lemon rind | Combine the pumpernickel crumbs, brown sugar, ground almonds and vanilla wafer crumbs in a large mixing bowl. Stir with a fork to press any lumps out of the sugar; blend thoroughly. Add the raisin mixture, grated orange rind and grated lemon rind. Blend with a fork. Stir in the melted butter. Cover the mixture and let stand for 3 hours. |
| 3 eggs<br>2 egg yolks | Beat the eggs and egg yolks until they are thick and lemon-colored. Stir into the pumpernickel mixture. |
| 4 egg whites<br>pinch cream of tartar<br>pinch salt | Beat the egg whites with the cream of tartar and salt until they hold stiff peaks. Stir one-fourth of the whites into the pumpernickel mixture, and fold in the remaining whites. |
| 1 cup heavy cream | Beat the cream in a chilled bowl until it holds stiff peaks. Fold the whipped cream into the pumpernickel mixture. Spoon the batter into the mold and cover with foil or a lid. Place on a rack in a deep kettle. Add enough boiling water to reach three-fourths of the way up the mold. Cover the kettle and steam the pudding, keeping the water at a boil, for 1½ hours. Add water as necessary to keep it at the same level. |
| sweetened whipped cream | Remove the mold from the kettle and let stand for 5 minutes. Place a heated platter over the mold and turn the pudding right side up onto the platter. Serve with sweetened whipped cream. |

## Filbert Balls

| | |
|---|---|
| 1¾-ounces semisweet chocolate | Melt the chocolate in the top of a double boiler. Remove from heat and stir to cool. |
| ¼ cup plus 2 tablespoons butter, softened<br>½ cup confectioners' sugar<br>the melted chocolate<br>½ cup plus 2 tablespoons filberts, ground | Beat the butter and sugar in a mixing bowl until the mixture is fluffy. Stir in the chocolate and beat until creamy and smooth. Stir in the ground filberts. Form the mixture into a ball. Wrap in waxed paper and chill for 30 minutes. |
| | Pinch off a teaspoonful of dough at a time, rolling it into a ball. Arrange the balls on a lightly greased and floured baking sheet. Bake in a preheated 300° oven for 8 minutes or until the balls have lost their gloss. Let cool on a baking sheet before serving. Makes about 30 balls. |

## Christmas Eve Menu for Six

Almond Soup
Avocado and Tomato Salad
Seafood Canalones with Parmesan Sauce
Baked Sea Bream
Turrón

*Spain*

1 3-pound stewing hen or parts
1 medium onion, quartered
2 celery ribs, sliced
2 carrots, sliced
1 clove garlic, crushed
2 tomatoes, quartered
½ green pepper, sliced
2 bay leaves
1 tablespoon salt
pinch saffron

¼ cup butter
¼ cup chopped almonds
¼ cup flour
2 cups hot chicken broth

½ cup heavy cream
½ cup milk
the stewing hen breast meat
¼ cup chopped pimientos
2 tablespoons chopped chives
2 tablespoons dry sherry

2 firm, ripe avocados
lime juice
3 tomatoes

3 tablespoons olive oil
2 tablespoons wine vinegar
1 tablespoon lime juice
1 tablespoon chopped parsley
½ teaspoon sugar
salt and pepper to taste

lettuce leaves
optional garnish:
3 hard-boiled eggs, chopped
Bermuda onion rings

### Almond Soup

For the chicken broth:
Place the whole hen or parts in a large kettle. Cover with 3 quarts cold water. Add the remaining ingredients. Be sure water covers the ingredients by a full inch. Bring to a simmer. Skim the surface as necessary. Lower the heat and simmer gently, partially covered, for 3 to 4 hours, adding more water if necessary. Remove stewing hen and reserve for another use. Strain the broth through a colander, pressing the vegetables with a wooden spoon to extract juices. Allow the broth to cool. Skim the fat from the surface. Pour 1½ quarts broth into a clean, 2½-quart kettle and bring to a simmer.

Melt the butter in a heavy skillet. Add the almonds, stirring frequently. Allow the almonds to brown lightly. Add the flour. Stir constantly for 2 minutes. Remove from the heat and add the hot broth. Beat with a wire whisk until smooth. Add the mixture to the remaining chicken broth. Cook, stirring, over moderate heat until the broth thickens. Simmer for 10 minutes more.

Stir the cream and milk into the broth mixture. Finely dice the breast meat and add to the broth. Add the pimientos and chives. Simmer ten minutes longer, stirring occasionally. Before serving, add the sherry and stir. Remove from heat immediately and serve.

### Avocado and Tomato Salad

Cut the avocados in half and remove the pits. Peel and cut into slices. Place the slices in a deep plate; sprinkle with the lime juice. Wash and slice the tomatoes into wedges.

For the dressing:
Combine the olive oil, wine vinegar, lime juice, parsley, sugar, salt and pepper in a small glass jar. Cover and shake well to blend. Refrigerate for 1 hour and let stand at room temperature 15 minutes before pouring.

Place a lettuce leaf on each of 6 salad plates. Arrange the tomato and avocado slices alternately in a pinwheel across the lettuce. Shake the salad dressing before pouring and coat each salad lightly. You may garnish with chopped hard-boiled eggs and a slice of onion if you wish.

## Seafood Canalones with Parmesan Sauce

For the canalones:
Combine the flour, milk, water, eggs, butter, salt, pepper and nutmeg in a large bowl. Beat until smooth with an electric or hand mixer. You can also mix in a blender until smooth. Let stand for 30 minutes.

Mix the butter and oil in a small cup. Place a 7-inch omelet or crepe pan over moderate heat. Use a basting brush to spread the butter and oil mixture onto the skillet. Spoon out enough batter to coat the bottom of the skillet (about 2 to 3 tablespoons); tilt the skillet to spread batter. Cook until a light, golden crust forms on the bottom and the batter is dry on the top. Flip the canalone over and cook a few seconds longer. Remove to a platter and continue cooking canalones until all batter has been used.

½ cup flour
½ cup milk
¼ cup water
4 eggs
1 tablespoon butter, melted
½ teaspoon salt
pinch each pepper and nutmeg
3 tablespoons butter, softened
2 tablespoons olive oil

For the filling:
Place the fish in a shallow baking dish. Add the cold water, wine and salt and bring to a simmer. Cover with a sheet of waxed paper. Set in a preheated 350° oven for 8 to 12 minutes or until the fish flakes easily when pierced with a fork. Allow the fish to cool completely in the dish. Remove the fish from the liquid and flake it into a bowl. Set the baking dish with the poaching liquid over moderate heat. Boil the liquid, reducing it to ¼ cup.

1 pound fillet red snapper, flounder, sole or crab meat
1½ cups cold water
¼ cup dry white wine
1 teaspoon salt

Heat the oil in a heavy skillet. Sauté the parsley and onion, stirring constantly for 8 minutes until the onion is soft. Add the chopped tomato and cook 5 minutes longer. Sprinkle in the flour and cook, stirring constantly, for 3 minutes. Remove from the heat and pour in the fish poaching liquid and the wine. Stir with a wire whisk until smooth. Add salt, pepper and nutmeg. Return to heat and stir until thickened. Add the flaked fish and blend thoroughly. Cool completely before using.

2 tablespoons olive oil
1 tablespoon chopped parsley
1 small onion, minced
1 tomato, seeded and chopped
2 tablespoons flour
the ¼ cup poaching liquid
2 tablespoons dry white wine
salt and pepper to taste
⅛ teaspoon nutmeg

## Parmesan Sauce:

Melt the butter in a heavy saucepan over low heat. Add the flour and cook, stirring constantly, until mixture just begins to turn golden. Remove from heat and pour in the milk. Beat with a wire whip until sauce is smooth. Return to heat and cook, stirring, until thick. Beat the egg yolk in a small bowl. Stir in a few drops of the hot white sauce. Continue to blend in gradually. When all the sauce has been added, return the mixture to the saucepan. Stir over low heat for 1 minute.

3 tablespoons butter
2 tablespoons flour
2 cups milk
1 egg yolk

Add the Parmesan cheese, nutmeg, salt, pepper and sherry to the white sauce. Simmer 2 minutes, stirring constantly. Remove from heat.

¼ cup grated Parmesan cheese
⅛ teaspoon nutmeg
salt and pepper to taste
2 tablespoons dry sherry

To prepare canalones:
Place 2 tablespoons of the filling along the center of each canalone. Roll up and place in a single layer in a buttered baking dish. Pour the Parmesan Sauce over the canalones and broil for 10 to 15 minutes until golden and bubbly.

## Baked Sea Bream

Have the fish cleaned and scaled at the market. Leave the fish whole. Make diagonal cuts at 1-inch intervals on one side of the fish. Place a lemon slice in each cut.

Combine the olive oil, sherry, onion, garlic, parsley, bay leaf, salt and pepper in a small glass jar. Cover and shake well to blend. Pour ¼ of the mixture into a shallow baking dish large enough to hold the fish. Lay the fish, cut side up, in the dish and pour the remaining mixture over it. Bake in a preheated 350° oven for 50 to 60 minutes. The fish is done when it just flakes when tested with a fork. Serve immediately.

1 3-pound sea bream (porgy or sea bass)
2 lemons, thinly sliced

3 tablespoons olive oil
½ cup dry sherry
¼ cup minced white onion
2 cloves garlic, minced
2 tablespoons minced parsley
1 bay leaf, crumbled
¼ teaspoon salt
¼ teaspoon pepper

## Turrón

Line a loaf pan with waxed paper cut to fit. Brush the waxed paper with vegetable oil. At the same time, prepare another piece of waxed paper brushed with oil and a piece of cardboard, both cut to fit just inside the pan.

a loaf pan
waxed paper
vegetable oil

Grind 1 cup of the almonds to a smooth paste in a blender, or crush with a mortar and pestle. Combine the remaining ½ cup whole almonds with the ground almonds.

1½ cups blanched almonds

Combine the sugar and water in a heavy-bottomed saucepan. Heat slowly until the sugar has completely dissolved. Increase the heat and boil 7 minutes. At this point, a few drops of sugar syrup should form hard balls when dropped into a bowl of cold water. Remove from the heat and add the almonds. Stir until the mixture forms a thick paste. It should come away from the sides of the pan as it is stirred. Add the egg yolks, stirring constantly. Press into the prepared pan and cover with the second piece of oiled waxed paper. Set the piece of cardboard on top of the waxed paper, securing it with a light weight on top. Set the loaf in a cool place.

1⅔ cups sugar
1⅛ cups cold water
4 egg yolks, beaten

Turn the loaf out of the pan. Remove the oiled papers. Cover the bottom of a plate with the sugar. Place the loaf topside down on the sugar. Turn the loaf right-side-up and set on a serving dish. Use a very hot skewer to burn a pattern of criss-cross lines in the top of the turrón.

¼ cup sugar

Avocado and Tomato Salad

*Stuffed Artichokes*
*Mushroom Salad   Antipasto Salad*
*Stuffed Pasta Shells with Tomato Sauce*
*Shrimp with Garlic and Parsley*
*Zabaglione   Panettone*

### Stuffed Artichokes

6 large artichokes
½ lemon
3 quarts boiling, salted water

Rinse artichokes under cold running water. Remove and discard any discolored outer leaves. Trim off ½ inch from the top of each leaf with a kitchen scissors to remove the sharp tips. Trim the stem end of each artichoke with a sharp knife, so that it will stand. Rub each artichoke with the lemon. Squeeze the remainder of juice into the boiling water. Drop the artichokes into the water and cook for 15 minutes. Drain, top side down, until cool enough to handle. Pull out the centers and scrape out the chokes with a small spoon.

1 cup dry bread crumbs
1 cup grated Romano cheese
8 cloves garlic, minced
4 tablespoons chopped parsley
salt and pepper to taste

Combine the bread crumbs, cheese, garlic, parsley, salt and pepper in a small bowl. Put ½ teaspoon of the mixture in the spaces between leaves, using a small spoon. Fill the centers with the remaining mixture. Arrange the artichokes in a pan just large enough to hold them.

3 tablespoons butter
2 tablespoons olive oil

Melt the butter in a small saucepan and add the olive oil. Put a few drops between the leaves of each artichoke to moisten the filling. Add ½-inch boiling water to the pan. Cover and bake in a preheated 400° oven for 1 hour, or until tender.

### Mushroom Salad

12 ounces fresh mushrooms

Rinse mushrooms quickly under cold running water, wiping them clean. Cut into thin slices and arrange in a salad bowl.

3 tablespoons olive oil
2 tablespoons lemon juice
1 tablespoon red wine vinegar
1 clove garlic, minced
½ teaspoon grated lemon rind
½ teaspoon sugar
pinch ground nutmeg
salt and pepper to taste
fresh parsley, chopped

Combine the olive oil, lemon juice, red wine vinegar, garlic, lemon rind, sugar, nutmeg, salt and pepper in a small glass jar. Cover and shake well to combine ingredients. Refrigerate for 1 hour. Let stand at room temperature for 15 minutes before serving. Shake the dressing again just before pouring over the mushrooms. Garnish the salad with the chopped parsley.

### Antipasto Salad

1 pound fresh green beans
2½ quarts boiling, salted water

Drop the beans into the boiling water. Cook for 8 minutes until tender but still crisp. Rinse under cold running water for 1 minute. Lay the beans out on a towel to dry. Roll up and refrigerate.

*Italy*

Combine the olive oil, lemon juice, red wine vinegar, onion, parsley, sugar, salt and pepper in a small glass jar. Cover and shake well to combine the ingredients. Refrigerate for 1 hour. Let stand at room temperature for 15 minutes before serving.

3 tablespoons olive oil
1½ tablespoons lemon juice
1½ tablespoons wine vinegar
1½ tablespoons minced onion
1½ tablespoons minced parsley
½ teaspoon sugar
salt and pepper to taste

Arrange the tomatoes around the edge of a serving platter. Fill the center of the platter with the green beans. Shake the dressing and pour over the beans and tomatoes evenly. Wrap the olives with the anchovy fillets for garnish.

3 tomatoes, sliced
12 to 16 pitted black olives, drained
12 to 16 anchovy fillets, drained

Thin the mayonnaise with a little cream or milk to pouring consistency. Spoon over the salad.

½ cup mayonnaise
cream or milk

### Stuffed Pasta Shells

Drop the shells into the boiling, salted water. Cook 15 to 20 minutes, testing occasionally. When the shells are tender but firm, drain in a colander under cold running water. Spread the shells in a single layer on a towel to dry.

1 12-ounce package jumbo pasta shells
6 quarts boiling, salted water

Cook the spinach according to package instructions, until most of the moisture has evaporated. Drain in a colander, pressing out any excess water.

2 10-ounce packages frozen spinach

For the filling:
Combine the ricotta cheese, spinach, Parmesan cheese, eggs, lemon juice, nutmeg, salt and pepper in a large bowl. Stir until well blended. Stuff each shell with the filling, distributing it evenly. Place the shells in a single layer in a buttered, shallow baking dish. Pour the tomato sauce on top. Bake in a preheated 350° oven 30 minutes, or until heated through.

1 15-ounce package ricotta cheese
the cooked spinach
½ cup Parmesan cheese
2 eggs
1 teaspoon lemon juice
pinch nutmeg
salt and pepper to taste

For the tomato sauce:
Heat the oil in a saucepan. Add the onion, garlic, celery, and carrot. Sauté slowly 10 minutes.

Peel, seed and chop the tomatoes. Add the tomatoes, tomato paste, wine, beef stock, water, sugar, nutmeg, salt and pepper. Bring to a boil, stirring. Lower the heat and simmer gently for 1 hour or until thickened, stirring occasionally.

Best when made a day ahead and refrigerated overnight.

2 tablespoons olive oil
1 onion, chopped
2 garlic cloves, minced
1 celery rib, chopped
1 carrot, grated
4 tomatoes
6-ounce can tomato paste
1 cup dry red wine
1 cup beef stock
1 cup water
1 tablespoon brown sugar
pinch nutmeg, salt and pepper

### Zabaglione

Combine the egg yolks and sugar in the top of a double boiler. Beat the mixture with a wire whisk over barely simmering water. Gradually add the wine when the mixture is lemon-colored and slightly thickened. Beat until thick and foamy. Add the vanilla. Remove from heat and beat a few minutes. Pour into six individual serving glasses. Serve immediately.

6 egg yolks
6 tablespoons sugar
½ cup Marsala wine
½ teaspoon vanilla

## Shrimp with Garlic and Parsley

Wash the shrimp under cold water. Peel and devein; lay on a towel to dry.

2½ to 3 pounds large shrimp

Heat the olive oil and butter in a large skillet. Place 1 layer of shrimp in the skillet. Season with salt and pepper. Sauté for 2 minutes. Turn and sauté for 1 minute. Transfer to a heated serving dish and keep warm. Sauté the remaining shrimp in the same manner.

3 tablespoons olive oil
3 tablespoons butter
salt and butter to taste

Add the garlic and parsley to the oil and butter remaining in the skillet. Heat and stir for a few seconds. Squeeze the lemon juice into the skillet. Pour sauce over the shrimp and serve.

4 cloves garlic, minced
½ cup minced parsley
juice of ½ lemon

## Panettone

Combine the water, sugar and salt in a small saucepan. Bring to a simmer, stirring, to dissolve sugar. Remove from heat and add butter. Stir to melt butter and cool to lukewarm.

1 cup water
½ cup sugar
2 teaspoons salt
½ cup butter

Combine the lukewarm water mixture and yeast in a large mixing bowl.  Stir to dissolve yeast. Add eggs, egg yolks, lemon peel and anise seed. Stir to combine thoroughly. Add flour and mix to form a smooth dough. Place on a floured board and knead, adding more flour if necessary until dough is smooth and satiny. Knead in the raisins, pine nuts and candied fruit.

2 packages active dry yeast
2 eggs, beaten
3 egg yolks, beaten
1 teaspoon grated lemon peel
1 teaspoon anise seed
5½ cups all-purpose flour
¾ cup raisins
¾ cup pine nuts
¾ cup mixed candied fruit

Place the dough in a lightly buttered bowl, turning to coat all sides. Cover with a towel and let rise in a warm place until doubled in bulk.

Deflate dough and knead again until smooth. Place in a greased 3-quart pudding pan or round pan. Cover and let rise until doubled in bulk. Cut a deep cross in the top of the loaf with a sharp knife or scissors.

Bake in a preheated 425° oven for about 8 minutes or until the surface begins to brown. Reduce temperature to 325° and bake about 1 hour longer. The bread is done when it is nicely browned and has a hollow sound when tapped.

Shrimp with Garlic and Parsley,
Stuffed Artichokes, Antipasto Salad

*Spinach Triangles*
*Lentil Soup*
*Beet and Onion Salad*
*Roast Stuffed Suckling Pig*
*Braised Celery    Glazed Carrots*
*Baklava*

## Spinach Triangles

⅓ cup olive oil
1 large onion, chopped
8 scallions, chopped
1½ pounds fresh spinach,
washed and chopped
3 tablespoons dried dillweed
1½ cups crumbled feta cheese
pepper to taste

½ pound phyllo pastry dough
olive oil

For the filling:
Heat the olive oil in a large saucepan. Add the onion and scallions. Cook over moderate heat, stirring until soft. Lay the spinach over the onion, cover and cook for 5 minutes. Stir the mixture to combine ingredients. Remove from heat. Add the dillweed, feta cheese and pepper; stir gently. Set aside to cool.

Cut the phyllo into 3 x 10-inch strips. Use the strips in double layers for each pastry. Place 1 tablespoon filling at one end of each strip. Fold one corner of the strip over the filling, forming a triangle. Continue to fold the pastry, maintaining the triangular shape (as you would fold a flag). Fill and fold each strip. Place the triangles on an oiled baking sheet. Brush with olive oil. Bake in a preheated 350° oven for 15 to 20 minutes until golden.

## Lentil Soup

1 pound dried lentil beans
1 onion, chopped
2 celery ribs, chopped
3 cloves garlic, minced
½ cup olive oil
2 tablespoons tomato paste
2 whole cloves
½ bay leaf
salt and pepper to taste

Rinse the lentil beans in a colander under cold running water. Soak for 1 hour in lukewarm water. Drain in a colander and transfer to a kettle. Add 2 quarts water, onion, celery, garlic, olive oil, tomato paste, cloves, bay leaf, salt and pepper. Bring to a boil over moderate heat. Reduce heat, cover and cook for 30 minutes. Check the soup occasionally, adding more water if necessary. Soup should be fairly thick. Pour into a heated tureen and serve.

## Beet and Onion Salad

2½ pounds medium-sized beets
1 tablespoon vinegar
1 tablespoon salt
1 large onion, sliced
salt and pepper to taste

Remove the leaves and stems from the beets. Wash under cold water. Place the beets in a kettle and cover with water. Add the vinegar and salt. Bring to a boil. Cover and cook for 45 minutes or until tender. Drain. When cooled slip off the skins by rubbing them between your fingers. Cut the beets crosswise into ¼-inch slices. Arrange the beets and onion in a salad bowl. Sprinkle with salt and pepper.

½ cup olive oil
2 tablespoons red wine vinegar
1 large clove garlic, split
½ teaspoon salt
¼ teaspoon pepper

The dressing:
Combine the olive oil, red wine vinegar, garlic, salt and pepper in a glass jar. Cover and shake to blend. Let stand at room temperature for 1 hour before serving. Dress the beet and onion slices generously.

*Greece*

# Roast Stuffed Suckling Pig

Have the piglet cleaned at the meat market. Wash the piglet and pat dry. Rub the cavity and outside with salt and pepper. Set aside.

1 12-pound piglet
salt and pepper

For the stuffing:
Combine the raisins and sherry in a small saucepan. Simmer for 3 minutes until the raisins are plump.

⅓ cup seedless raisins
⅓ cup sherry

Heat the olive oil in a large heavy-bottomed skillet over moderate heat. Add the onion and sauté for 5 minutes. Add the ground pork, breaking it up as it cooks. After the meat has browned lightly, add the rice, raisins, pine nuts, parsley, sage, salt and pepper. Pour in the water and cook, stirring occasionally, for 15 minutes. The rice should be half cooked with the water absorbed. Remove from the heat. Cool before using.

3 tablespoons olive oil
3 tablespoons chopped onion
¾ pound ground pork
¾ cup uncooked rice
the plump raisins
½ cup pine nuts
½ cup chopped parsley
2 tablespoons sage
salt and pepper to taste
1 cup water

Fill the piglet loosely with the stuffing. Close the cavity with skewers and lace with kitchen string. Pull the front legs forward and tie them together. Do the same with the back legs. Place the piglet in the roasting pan, stomach down. Brush with olive oil. Make a few small, shallow cuts in the piglet's back with a sharp knife. Place the block of wood in the mouth to keep it open. Cover the ears with foil so they do not burn. Pour boiling water into the pan. Roast in a preheated 350° oven, basting occasionally with olive oil. Figure 30 minutes roasting time for every pound of meat. If the skin should begin to brown too quickly, cover loosely with aluminum foil. Uncover the piglet during the last 30 minutes of roasting to allow the skin to become crisp. When the piglet has finished cooking, remove to a warm platter. Cover loosely to keep warm.

the prepared piglet
skewers
kitchen string
olive oil
basting brush
1 small block of wood
foil
shallow roasting pan
2 cups boiling water

For the gravy:
Skim all but 2 tablespoons of the fat from the pan juice. Bring the juice to a simmer. Sprinkle the flour on the juice and stir until bubbly (2 minutes). Add the water, stirring constantly. Simmer until thickened. Season with salt and pepper. Serve in a warm sauceboat.

2 tablespoons flour
2½ cups water
salt and pepper to taste

# Braised Celery

Remove the core and fibrous outer ribs from each bunch of celery. Trim off the tops, leaving the ribs 6 to 8 inches long. Quarter each rib. Rinse the celery under cold running water. Place in a saucepan, cover with water, and add the salt. Bring to a boil. Blanch the celery for 5 minutes. Drain in a colander.

2 bunches pascal celery
1 tablespoon salt

Heat the olive oil in a shallow casserole dish. Add the carrot and onion. Sauté over moderate heat for 8 to 10 minutes. Place the celery on top of the vegetables. Pour in the chicken stock. Add salt and pepper. Bring to a boil. Reduce heat, cover and simmer gently for 30 to 45 minutes. Celery should be tender. Remove celery with a slotted spoon to a heated serving dish and keep warm.

2 tablespoons olive oil
1 carrot, chopped
1 small onion, chopped
¾ cup chicken stock
salt and pepper to taste
2 tablespoons chopped, fresh
 flat-leaf parsley

Strain the chopped carrots and onion from the casserole; force the carrots and onion through a sieve back into the stock. Pour it over the cooked celery. Sprinkle with parsley and serve.

## Glazed Carrots

1 pound small young carrots, peeled

½ cup cold water
2 tablespoons butter
2 tablespoons sugar
1 bouillon cube
pinch pepper

If the carrots are small and garden fresh, they may be left whole. If not, slice them lengthwise into quarters, then crosswise in half.

Place the carrots in a heavy saucepan. Add the water, butter, sugar and bouillon cube. Simmer gently, partially covered, until liquid is reduced to 2 tablespoons. Uncover and simmer until liquid becomes a glaze. Shake the pan, coating the carrots evenly with glaze.

## Baklava

1½ cups walnuts, chopped
1½ cups walnuts, ground
¾ cups almonds, chopped
2 teaspoons ground cinnamon
¾ teaspoon ground cloves

1 pound unsalted butter, melted
1 pound phyllo pastry

For the filling:
Combine the chopped and ground walnuts, chopped almonds, cinnamon and cloves. Set aside.

Cut the layers of phyllo dough to fit a 9 x 12-inch baking pan. Set aside 4 layers for the top. Keep the phyllo dough covered at all times with a damp dish towel. It will dry quickly if exposed to the air. Brush the baking pan with the melted butter. Lay a sheet of phyllo in the pan and brush with butter. Sprinkle evenly with a handful of the nut mixture. Repeat this layering process until all the nuts are used. Lay the 4 remaining phyllo sheets on top, brushing each generously with melted butter. Using the tip of a sharp knife, cut a diamond-shaped pattern through the top 4 layers, leaving about 2 inches between each cut. Bake for 45 minutes in a preheated 325° oven until the top turns golden. Remove from the oven and cool slightly.

2 cups sugar
1¼ cups water
peel of 1 orange
4 whole cloves
1 cinnamon stick
6 ounces honey
juice of ½ lemon
½ teaspoon vanilla
¼ teaspoon almond extract

For the syrup:
Combine the sugar, water, orange peel, cloves and cinnamon stick in a saucepan. Simmer for 2 minutes. Add the honey and lemon juice. Boil for 5 minutes. Remove from the heat. Stir in the vanilla and almond extract. Allow to cool. Pour the syrup evenly over the baklavas. Cut through all the dough layers following the diamond-shaped pattern made earlier. Let stand overnight before serving.

Beet and Onion Salad, Braised Celery, Glazed Carrots, Spinach Triangles, Baklava

# Christmas Day Menu for Six

## Christmas Cheese Ball
## Fish Soup
## Paprika Chicken
## Noodles and Cabbage
## Chestnut Torte

**Hungary**

### Christmas Cheese Ball

2 8-ounce packages cream cheese, softened
⅔ cup crumbled blue cheese

Place the cream cheese in a large mixing bowl. Spread the cream cheese around the bowl with a heavy fork to allow it to soften. Add the blue cheese and blend well.

3 tablespoons sweet sherry
1 tablespoon Worcestershire sauce
1 clove garlic, finely minced
3 tablespoons minced chives
1 tablespoon caraway seeds
1½ cups finely minced parsley

Blend the sherry, and Worcestershire sauce into the cheese. Add the minced garlic, chives and caraway seeds. Blend all the ingredients together with a fork. Roll the mixture into a ball with your hands. Spread the minced parsley on a plate. Roll the cheese ball in the parsley, coating it completely. Wrap the ball in waxed paper and refrigerate for at least 4 hours or overnight.

1 7-ounce jar pimientos
pearl onions
stuffed green olives
toothpicks

Lay the pimientos on a cutting board. With a sharp knife, cut out decorations. Attach pimiento decorations onto the cheese ball with the toothpicks. Place pearl onions or olives on the ends of the toothpicks.

### Fish Soup

2 pounds pike, sturgeon, halibut or flounder
1½ cups bottled clam juice
1 onion, thinly sliced
8 parsley stems
1 teaspoon lemon juice
¼ cup fresh mushroom stems
5 peppercorns
5½ cups cold water

Put the fish in a large heavy-bottomed kettle. Add the clam juice, sliced onion, parsley stems, lemon juice, mushroom stems and peppercorns. Cover with the cold water and slowly bring to a simmer. Simmer very gently, uncovered for 30 minutes. Strain the broth through a sieve and pour it into a large saucepan over low heat. When the fish is cool enough to handle, remove all the bones and break the fish into pieces. Cover the fish with foil and set aside.

3 tablespoons butter
3 tablespoons flour
6 cups of the simmering fish stock

Wash the kettle and place it over low heat. Melt the butter in the kettle. Add the flour, stirring over moderate heat for 3 minutes. Remove from the heat. Pour in the hot fish stock, stirring with a wire whisk to blend the stock thoroughly with the flour. Cook the soup over low heat until it thickens slightly. Simmer, stirring occasionally for 10 minutes.

¼ cup sour cream
¼ cup rice

Beat in the sour cream with the wire whisk. Rinse the rice in a sieve under cold running water and add to the soup. Partially cover the kettle. Simmer until the rice is tender, stirring occasionally.

the fish meat
lemon slices

Divide the fish meat among 6 heated soup bowls. Ladle the simmering soup over the fish. Garnish each bowl with a slice of lemon floating on top.

## Paprika Chicken

Rinse the chicken under cold running water. Pat dry thoroughly with a paper towel. Salt and pepper lightly and set aside.

Heat the butter in a Dutch oven. Add the onion and sauté for 8 minutes, stirring occasionally. Remove from the heat.

Add the paprika, chicken pieces, green pepper, tomato and water to the Dutch oven. Stir to combine ingredients and cover tightly. Return to the heat and simmer slowly for 1 to 1½ hours, turning the chicken once during cooking. Or bring to a simmer on top of stove and place in a preheated 325° oven for 1 to 1½ hours.

During the last 15 minutes of cooking time, add the sliced mushrooms. Cover and return to the oven.

When the chicken is tender, transfer it to a heated platter. Remove the vegetables with a slotted spoon and spoon over the chicken. Add the butter to the Dutch oven and set over low heat. Stir in the flour; continue stirring for 2 minutes. Remove from heat and pour in all the chicken broth at once, beating vigorously with a wire whisk until the sauce is smooth. Return to heat and stir occasionally while the sauce simmers, for 5 to 10 minutes. If the sauce becomes too thick, thin it with a little water. If it is too thin, continue to simmer until more liquid evaporates.

Blend the sour cream into the sauce, stirring until heated through. Do not allow the sauce to simmer or it will curdle. Spoon the sauce over the chicken. Garnish the platter with green pepper and tomato slices.

**2½ to 3 pounds chicken, cut into serving pieces**
**salt and pepper to taste**

**6 tablespoons butter**
**1 large onion, sliced**

**2 tablespoons Hungarian paprika**
**the cut up chicken**
**½ green pepper, sliced**
**½ ripe tomato, sliced**
**⅓ cup cold water**

**¼ pound fresh mushrooms, cleaned and sliced**

**2 tablespoons butter**
**3 tablespoons flour**
**1½ cups boiling chicken broth**

**⅓ cup sour cream**
**½ green pepper, sliced**
**½ ripe tomato, sliced**

## Noodles and Cabbage

Melt the butter in a large heavy skillet. Add the onion and sauté for 8 to 10 minutes or until the onion is soft but not browned.

Remove any discolored leaves and quarter the cabbage, cutting out the core. Shred to measure 4 cups. Add to the skillet and sauté for 5 minutes until crisp and tender. Stir in the caraway seed; salt and pepper to taste.

Cook the noodles in salted water according to package directions. Drain well. Stir noodles into the cabbage. Add sour cream. Stir frequently for 5 minutes over low heat until heated through. Do not allow mixture to boil or the sour cream will curdle. Serve immediately.

**¼ cup butter**
**½ cup chopped onion**

**4 cups shredded cabbage**
**1 teaspoon caraway seed**
**salt and pepper to taste**

**1 8-ounce package egg noodles**
**½ cup sour cream**

## Chestnut Torte

Place the chestnuts in a pan and cover with cold water. Bring to a boil for 1 minute. Remove from heat. Remove 3 chestnuts at a time from the pan. Peel off shells and inner skins.

Put the chestnuts in a pan and pour in enough milk to cover by 1 inch. Simmer slowly, uncovered, 45 to 60

**1 pound chestnuts**

**milk as needed**

minutes until the chestnuts are cooked through. Drain in a colander and press through a fine sieve. Set aside.

1 9-inch round cake pan
shortening
2 tablespoons flour
waxed paper

Grease the cake pan with the shortening. Add the flour coating the pan evenly. Cut a circle of waxed paper large enough to fit the bottom of the pan. Grease the waxed paper and dust it with flour.

6 egg whites
pinch salt
pinch cream of tartar
⅓ cup sugar

Beat the egg whites with the salt until foamy. Add the cream of tartar and beat until soft peaks form. Gradually add the sugar and continue beating until stiff peaks are formed. Set aside.

6 egg yolks
⅔ cup sugar
the beaten egg whites
the chestnut puree
1 tablespoon fine bread crumbs

Beat the egg yolks until light. Add the sugar and continue beating 2 to 3 minutes. Stir ¼ of the egg whites into egg yolk mixture with a rubber spatula. Place half the chestnut puree on top of the egg yolk mixture. Sprinkle on half the bread crumbs. Add half of the egg white mixture. Fold together. Repeat with the remaining ingredients.

Pour the batter into the cake pan, spreading to the rim. Bake in a preheated 350° oven 25 to 30 minutes. Cool on a wire rack 5 minutes. Invert the cake onto the wire rack and peel off the waxed paper.

1 16-ounce can peeled apricots in heavy syrup
⅓ cup sugar

For the filling:
Drain the apricot syrup into a saucepan. Add the sugar. Bring to a simmer and stir to dissolve the sugar. Boil rapidly until thick and sticky.

the drained apricots
1 tablespoon lemon juice
½ teaspoon grated lemon rind

Remove the seeds from the apricots. Dice and stir into the syrup. Add the lemon juice and rind. Boil slowly for 5 minutes.

1 tablespoon kirsch or orange-flavored liqueur

Remove the saucepan from the heat and add the kirsch or orange-flavored liqueur. Let the mixture cool before spreading. Split the cake evenly into 2 layers. Invert the bottom layer onto a serving dish. Place pieces of waxed paper under the cake to catch any drippings. Pour the apricot filling onto the bottom layer and spread evenly to the edge. Set the second cake layer on top of the first. Spread the remaining filling around the sides.

3 ounces semisweet chocolate
1½ tablespoons vegetable oil

For the chocolate topping:
Break the chocolate into pieces and put in the top of a double boiler set over simmering water. Pour in the oil. Cover for 5 to 10 minutes until the chocolate melts. Stir to blend and pour over the cake.

12 ounces almonds, sliced
maraschino cherries, halved
whole blanched almonds

Gently press the sliced almonds into the glaze around the sides of the cake until completely coated. Decorate the top with the maraschino cherries and blanched whole almonds.

Czechoslovakia

Christmas Day
Menu for Six

Oxtail Soup
Prague Salad
Sautéed Mushrooms    Creamed Cabbage
Roast Pork    Potato Dumplings
Stuffed Baked Apples    Kolacky

### Oxtail Soup

1½ pounds oxtail
2 quarts water

Cut the oxtail into 1-inch pieces. Bring water to a boil in a large kettle. Drop the meat into the water; return to a boil. Skim the surface with a large spoon as necessary. Lower heat and simmer, partially covered, for 2 hours or until tender.

3 tablespoons butter
2 parsnips, diced
3 carrots, diced
1 medium onion, diced
5 peppercorns

Heat the butter in a skillet. Add the parsnips, carrots and onion and sauté 10 minutes or until vegetables are soft, but not browned. Add the vegetables and peppercorns to the soup. Simmer 10 minutes. With a slotted spoon, remove the oxtail pieces from the soup. Remove the meat from the bones and return the meat to the soup. Remove and discard peppercorns.

salt
3 cups diced cauliflower
2 tablespoons minced parsley

Taste the soup for seasoning, adding salt if necessary. Add cauliflower and parsley; simmer 15 minutes. Serve immediately.

### Prague Salad

½ cup cooked pork strips
½ cup cooked veal strips
1 cup sliced yellow onion
1 cup thinly sliced pickles
2 cups thinly sliced tart apples

For the salad:
Cut the pork and veal into strips 2 inches long by ½ inch wide by ⅛ inch thick. Combine the pork, veal, onion, pickles and apples in a mixing bowl.

1 cup mayonnaise
2 tablespoons cream
1 tablespoon lemon juice
salt and pepper
Romaine lettuce leaves

For the dressing:
Combine the mayonnaise, cream, lemon juice, salt and pepper in a small bowl. Blend thoroughly. Pour the dressing over the salad and toss to coat the ingredients. Refrigerate 4 hours. Arrange a bed of lettuce in a salad bowl. Place the salad on the lettuce leaves and serve.

### Sautéed Mushrooms

¼ cup butter
2 cups sliced red onion
1½ pounds mushrooms, sliced
salt and pepper
1 teaspoon caraway seed

Heat the butter in a heavy skillet. Add onion and sauté for 5 minutes or until soft. Add mushrooms, salt and pepper to taste and caraway seed. Sauté for 10 minutes. Serve immediately.

### Creamed Cabbage

1 large head of cabbage
¾ cup minced onion
5 tablespoons butter

Remove outer leaves from cabbage and discard. Cut cabbage into quarters, core and shred. In a large skillet, sauté cabbage and onion in butter for 5 minutes. Cover tightly and simmer until vegetables are just limp.

Sprinkle vegetables with salt and pepper. Blend cream into flour and add to vegetables. Stir to blend thoroughly. Cover and simmer for 10 to 15 minutes or until tender.

salt and pepper to taste
1 cup heavy cream
1 tablespoon flour

## Potato Dumplings

Drop the unpeeled potatoes into the boiling water. Cook until tender. Pour off hot water and cover the potatoes with cold water. Let stand until cool enough to handle. Peel and mash.

4 pounds potatoes
4 quarts boiling water

Add the water to a kettle and return to the heat; bring to a boil. In the meantime prepare the dumplings. Add flour, farina, eggs and salt to mashed potatoes. Mix into a stiff dough. To test the dough, form one small walnut-sized ball and drop it into the boiling water. If it falls apart, work more flour into the dough. Form the dough into 10 dumplings and drop immediately into the boiling water. Cook 15 minutes, stirring to prevent sticking.

4 quarts water
1⅓ cups flour
1 cup farina
2 eggs
2 teaspoons salt

## Roast Pork

Rub the roast with the garlic. Combine the seasonings in a small dish; rub into the meat. Sprinkle the roast with the caraway seed.

4-pound loin of pork
1 clove garlic, halved
¼ teaspoon each rosemary, allspice, sage, thyme
salt and pepper
1 teaspoon caraway seed

Place the meat in a glass dish. Cover loosely and let stand at room temperature for 1 hour before roasting.

Place the roast, fat side up, on a rack in a shallow roasting pan. Place in a preheated 450° oven. Immediately reduce heat to 325° and roast, basting occasionally, for 1 hour and 45 minutes. A meat thermometer inserted in the thickest part should register 175°. Transfer the pork to a heated platter and cover loosely while preparing the gravy.

Skim all but 2 tablespoons of fat from the roasting pan. Sprinkle on the flour and stir over moderately low heat for 2 to 3 minutes without browning. Add the water and milk. Stir with a wire whisk until the mixture is smooth and thickened. Add the brown sugar, salt, pepper and allspice. Transfer the gravy to a heated sauceboat and serve with the roast.

2 tablespoons flour
½ cup water
½ cup milk
½ teaspoon brown sugar
salt and pepper to taste
pinch allspice

## Stuffed Baked Apples

Combine the raisins and rum in a saucepan. Bring to a simmer. Remove from heat and let stand for 30 minutes.

½ cup chopped raisins
¼ cup dark rum

Cut the tops off the apples and reserve. Core the apples but do not peel. Rub lemon juice over the cut surfaces of the apples to prevent discoloration.

6 large baking apples
lemon juice

Combine and blend the ground hazelnuts, cream, raisins and sugar in a mixing bowl. Stuff the apples with the mixture and cover with the reserved apple tops. Place apples close together in a deep baking dish.

1 cup ground hazelnuts
½ cup heavy cream
the raisins soaked in rum
½ cup sugar

Combine the honey and rum. Pour over the apples. Bake for 30 to 35 minutes in a preheated 400° oven, basting the apples often. Serve with whipped cream.

½ cup honey
½ cup dark rum
sweetened whipped cream

## Kolacky

For the dough:
Scald the milk in a small saucepan. Remove from heat. Add sugar, shortening and salt. Stir to melt shortening. Cool to lukewarm.

Combine the lukewarm milk mixture and yeast in a large mixing bowl. Stir to dissolve yeast. Add the eggs and stir well. Add flour and mix to form a smooth dough. Shape into a ball and knead until smooth and satiny. Place in a lightly buttered bowl, turning to coat all sides. Cover with a towel and let rise in a warm place until doubled in size.

For the apricot filling:
Combine the apricots and water in a small saucepan. Simmer for 15 minutes or until the apricots are soft. Press the apricots and liquid through a sieve and return to the saucepan. Continue to simmer until thickened.

Add sugar, stirring occasionally over moderate heat for 5 minutes. Remove from heat. Cool before using.

For the prune filling:
Combine the prunes and water in a saucepan. Cover and simmer for 5 minutes. Remove from heat. Transfer the prunes to a colander. When cool enough to handle, pit the prunes. Return the prunes to the liquid in the saucepan. Simmer, uncovered, for 15 minutes. Press the mixture through a sieve and return to the saucepan; add the sugar. Continue to simmer over moderate heat until thickened, about 5 minutes. Cool before using.

Roll the dough into 1-inch balls. Place each ball on a greased cookie sheet and flatten to make a 2-inch circle. Make an indentation in the center, leaving a ¼-inch rim. Fill with apricot or prune filling. Allow the pastries to rise until doubled in size. Bake in a preheated 350° oven for 25 to 30 minutes. Sprinkle with confectioners' sugar while still warm.

1 cup milk
3 tablespoons sugar
¼ cup shortening
1 teaspoon salt

1 package active dry yeast
2 eggs, beaten
4⅓ cups all-purpose flour

½ pound dried apricots
1½ cups water

⅓ cup sugar

1 pound dried prunes
1½ cups water
1 tablespoon sugar

the apricot or prune filling
confectioners' sugar

Apricot and Prune-Filled Kolacky,
Stuffed Baked Apples

43

*Christmas Eve
Menu for Six*

*Christmas Barshch
Herring and Apple Salad
Carp in Beer Sauce
Stewed Sauerkraut with Mushrooms
Cranberry Pudding     Poppy Seed Cake*

### Christmas Barshch

1½ cups fish heads, bones, tails
or leftovers
3 carrots, sliced
2 celery ribs, sliced
2 onions, sliced
¼ head cabbage, shredded
1 clove garlic, halved
2 sprigs parsley

Combine the fish, carrots, celery, onion, cabbage, garlic and parsley in a heavy kettle. Cover with 2 quarts cold water. Bring to a simmer, keeping the heat low so the liquid never comes to a rolling boil. Simmer the stock gently, partially covered, for 1 hour. Strain the stock through a sieve, pressing the fish and vegetables with a wooden spoon to extract as much juice as possible. Discard the fish parts and vegetables.

8 medium beets
the fish stock
pinch allspice
1 tablespoon lemon juice
1 teaspoon sugar
salt and pepper to taste

Wash the beets under cold running water. Place the beets in a shallow baking pan. Bake for 30 minutes in a preheated 350° oven. Remove from the oven and let the beets set until cool enough to handle. Peel beets by rubbing the skins between your fingers. Grate coarsely. Add to the soup. Add allspice. Simmer for 5 minutes. Add the lemon juice and sugar. Taste for seasoning, adding salt and pepper if necessary.

### Herring and Apple Salad

1 pound salt herring

Have herring cleaned, skinned and filleted at the market. Cut each herring diagonally into 2 pieces.

2 medium apples
1 tablespoon lemon juice
1 small mild onion, minced

Peel and grate the apples. Sprinkle grated apples with the lemon juice and toss to coat. Add minced onion.

¼ cup heavy cream
1 tablespoon sugar
½ cup sour cream
¼ teaspoon horseradish
salt to taste
lettuce or cabbage leaves
tomato or carrot slices
slices of leek

In a chilled bowl beat the cream and sugar until mixture holds a peak. Beat in the sour cream, horseradish and salt to taste. Pour into the apple-onion mixture and blend thoroughly.

Place a lettuce or cabbage leaf on each salad plate. Divide the apple-onion mixture among the plates. Place the pieces of herring on top and garnish with a tomato or carrot slice and a slice of leek.

### Carp in Beer Sauce

1 4-pound carp

Have the fish cleaned and scaled at the market. Wash the fish in cold water and pat dry. Salt fish and let stand for 1 hour before cooking.

2½ tablespoons butter
1 large onion, chopped

Heat the butter in a heavy skillet over moderate heat. Add the onion and sauté for 2 minutes.

Add the sliced lemon, sugar, bay leaf, juniper berries and pepper to taste. Stir in the beer and simmer for 20 minutes. Strain the mixture through a sieve into a bowl. Discard the lemon slices, bay leaf and juniper berries. Pour the liquid into a pan large enough to poach the fish.

1 lemon, sliced
2 teaspoons sugar
½ bay leaf
4 juniper berries
pepper
2 cups dark beer or lager

Add the raisins and gingersnaps to the fish poaching pan. Cook the sauce over moderate heat until the crumbs have softened.

¼ cup golden raisins
¼ cup crushed gingersnaps

Place the carp in the pan. Bring the sauce to a simmer. Cover with a sheet of waxed paper and a lid. Poach the fish over moderately low heat for 15 to 20 minutes or until the fish just flakes when tested with a fork. Transfer the fish to a heated serving platter using 2 slotted spatulas to keep fish from breaking apart. Pour sauce over the fish and garnish with minced parsley and tomato quarters.

the carp
minced fresh parsley
2 tomatoes, quartered

## Stewed Sauerkraut with Mushrooms

Soak the dried mushrooms in the water for 1 hour; slice. If using fresh mushrooms, slice and simmer in 3 tablespoons water for 5 minutes. Drain and reserve cooking liquid.

1 ounce dried mushrooms
   or ¼ pound fresh
½ cup water

If sauerkraut is uncooked, rinse and drain. Place in a kettle and cover with boiling water. Boil, partially covered, for 30 minutes. Drain the sauerkraut in a colander and press out any excess liquid.

1½ pounds sauerkraut

In a large skillet cook the mushrooms and onion in the shortening for 5 minutes over moderate heat. When the onions are soft, add the flour and reduce the heat, stirring constantly for 2 minutes. Remove from heat and pour in the mushroom liquid and a little water to make a thick, smooth paste. Stir in the sauerkraut. Add salt and pepper to taste. Cook the mixture, stirring, until heated through.

1 large onion, chopped
2 tablespoons shortening
2 tablespoons flour
the reserved mushroom liquid
the mushrooms
a few tablespoons water
salt and pepper to taste

## Cranberry Pudding

Combine the cranberries and cold water in a saucepan. Bring to a simmer, and cook slowly just until the skins pop. Remove from the heat and run through a fine sieve or puree in a blender. Return to the saucepan. Add the sugar and stir to dissolve.

1 pound cranberries
1¼ cups cold water
½ cup sugar

Blend the cornstarch with the cold water in a small bowl. Stir into the cranberries and bring to a boil, stirring. Remove from heat and cool. Pour into a serving bowl or individual serving glasses. Spoon whipped cream on top and serve.

¼ cup cornstarch
¼ cup cold water
whipped cream

## Poppy Seed Cake

Combine the yeast, sugar and milk in a small bowl. Stir to dissolve the sugar and let stand for 5 minutes. Stir in the flour, cover, and let stand in a warm place until double in size.

1 package active dry yeast
2 tablespoons sugar
1 cup lukewarm milk
1 cup all-purpose flour

In a large bowl, beat the eggs and the egg yolks until they are blended. Add the sugar gradually while beating. Continue beating for 2 to 3 minutes. The mixture should turn a pale yellow.

Add the flour, yeast mixture, vanilla and lemon rind. Knead the dough for 5 minutes. Add the butter a little at a time. Knead 5 minutes longer until smooth. Place the dough in a large buttered bowl, turning to coat on all sides with butter. Cover with a towel and place in a warm 100° oven with the door ajar until double in size.

For the filling:
Combine the milk and sugar in a saucepan. Bring the mixture to a boil over moderate heat. Stir to dissolve sugar completely. Stir in the poppy seed, raisins, orange and lemon rind. Remove from heat. Let the mixture cool completely before using.

Beat the egg whites lightly and fold into the poppy seed mixture. Stir in the butter.

When the dough has doubled in size, punch it down and roll into a 24 x 14-inch rectangle. Spread with the poppy seed filling, except 1 inch around the edge. Beginning with a long side, roll up the dough jelly-roll fashion. Arrange roll, seam side down, on a buttered baking sheet. Let it rise, loosely covered, in a warm place for 1 hour.

Brush the roll with water and bake in a preheated 350° oven for 45 minutes. Cool on a rack while preparing the glaze.

Beat the confectioners' sugar, lemon juice, boiling water and vanilla in a small bowl until the mixture is light and fluffy. Spread on the cooled cake. Let the cake stand until the glaze has set.

## Apricot and Prune Compote

Rinse the fruit and place in a bowl. Cover with the water and let soak for 24 hours.

Transfer the fruit to a serving bowl. Pour the liquid into a saucepan. Add the sugar. Cook, stirring, over low heat until the sugar is dissolved. Remove from the heat. Add the lemon juice and rind. Pour over the fruit and refrigerate.

---

1 egg
3 egg yolks
½ cup plus 1 tablespoon sugar
3½ cups all-purpose flour
the yeast mixture
1 teaspoon vanilla
1 teaspoon grated lemon rind
¼ pound butter, melted

1 cup milk
1 cup sugar
½ pound ground poppy seed
⅓ cup raisins
1½ teaspoons grated orange rind
1½ teaspoons grated lemon rind

2 egg whites, lightly beaten
2 tablespoons softened butter

2 cups confectioners' sugar
2 tablespoons lemon juice
1½ tablespoons boiling water
1 teaspoon vanilla

¼ pound dried apricots
¼ pound prunes
2 cups water

1 cup sugar
1 tablespoon lemon juice
grated rind from 1 lemon

Christmas Barshch,
Herring and Apple Salad

47

## Christmas Day Menu for Six

*Caviar-Stuffed Eggs*
*Eggplant Zakuski with Black Bread*
*Cucumber and Radish Salad*
*Roast Duck with Madeira Sauce*
*Veal Stuffing   Roast Potatoes*
*Buttered Cauliflower and Green Peas*
*Raisin and Almond Mazurka*

### Caviar-Stuffed Eggs

6 eggs
4 tablespoons red or black caviar

Boil the eggs for 8 minutes. Rinse under cold water. Peel the eggs; cut in half lengthwise. Remove the yolks, press through sieve and reserve. Divide the caviar among the egg white halves.

mayonnaise
2 tomatoes, quartered
6 green onions
fresh parsley or dill
the sieved egg yolks

Spoon some mayonnaise into a small serving bowl. Place the bowl in the middle of a large round platter. Surround the bowl with tomato wedges. Arrange the caviar-stuffed eggs around the tomatoes. Peel and slice the green onions. Garnish with the green onion, parsley or dill and sieved egg yolks.

### Eggplant Zakuski with Black Bread

2 medium eggplants
olive oil

Wash the eggplants and score with a fork. Brush with the oil. Bake in a preheated 350° oven 30 minutes, until tender. Cut the eggplants in half lengthwise and remove all the pulp, discarding peels. Chop very fine. Drain.

¼ cup olive oil
2 tablespoons wine vinegar
2 tablespoons lemon juice
1 clove garlic, minced
sugar, salt and pepper to taste

For the dressing:
Combine the olive oil, wine vinegar, lemon juice, garlic, sugar, salt and pepper in a jar. Cover and shake to blend the ingredients. Refrigerate for 1 hour. Let stand at room temperature for 15 minutes before serving.

1 medium onion, minced
1 green pepper, minced
2 tomatoes, seeded and minced
the dressing
small pieces of buttered black bread

Combine the onion, pepper and tomatoes in a bowl. Pour in the dressing. Add the prepared eggplant. Blend the mixture thoroughly. If the mixture is too moist for spreading, simmer it slowly in a saucepan to evaporate moisture. Chill thoroughly. Place in a serving bowl, and serve with the buttered black bread.

### Cucumber and Radish Salad

1 fresh cucumber
2 bunches radishes
salt

Wash the cucumber. Score the cucumber with a fork. Cut into thin slices. Salt lightly. Set aside. Trim the radishes. Wash and cut into thin slices. Arrange the cucumber and radish slices in a shallow salad bowl. Coat evenly with the sour cream dressing.

6 tablespoons sour cream
1 tablespoon wine vinegar
1 tablespoon lemon juice
½ teaspoon sugar
pinch salt

For the dressing:
Combine the sour cream, wine vinegar, lemon juice, sugar and salt in a jar. Cover and shake to blend the ingredients. Refrigerate for 1 hour. Let stand at room temperature for 15 minutes before serving.

## Roast Duck with Madeira Sauce

Wash the duck under cold running water. Pat dry with a towel. Salt the inside and outside of the duck.

| |
|---|
| 1 5-pound duck |
| salt |

The veal stuffing:
Remove the crust from the bread and reserve for another use. Cut the bread into ½-inch cubes. Place the bread cubes in a large baking pan. Set in a preheated 300° oven for 20 minutes, turning the cubes occasionally. Transfer the dried cubes to a bowl and soak with milk. Press out any excess milk and set aside.

½ loaf stale white bread, such as Vienna or Italian
1 cup milk

Heat the butter until foaming in a large heavy skillet. Add the onion and sauté for 5 minutes. Beat the eggs with the water in a small bowl. Pour into the skillet. Scramble the eggs with the onion. Set aside.

1½ tablespoons butter
1 large onion, chopped
2 eggs
2 tablespoons cold water

Chop the veal coarsely. Put the veal, bread, and scrambled eggs with onion in a food processor to blend. Or put the ingredients through a meat grinder and combine in a large bowl. Add the scrambled eggs and onion, salt, pepper and nutmeg. Stir to blend.

1 pound cooked veal
the milk-soaked bread
the scrambled eggs and onion
1 egg
salt, pepper and nutmeg to taste

Stuff the body and neck cavities of the bird loosely with the veal stuffing. Close the cavity with skewers and lace with kitchen string. Close the neck cavity with a skewer. Truss the bird securely with the string so it will keep its shape while roasting. Pierce through the skin around the thighs, back and lower breast with a fork so the fat will drain during roasting. Place the duck, breast side up, on a rack in a shallow roasting pan. Set the pan in the middle level of a preheated 425° oven for 15 minutes to brown the skin lightly. Reduce the heat to 350° and turn the bird on one side. Remove fat occasionally from the pan with a bulb baster. The duck will not need to be basted. After 30 minutes turn the bird on the other side. Figure 15 minutes roasting time for every pound of meat. To test whether the bird is done, pierce the thigh with a small knife. If the juice is rosy-colored, roast another 5 to 10 minutes. When done, discard the trussing strings and skewers. Scoop stuffing into a heated serving bowl. Set the duck on a heated platter, cover loosely and keep warm.

the duck, cleaned and salted
the veal stuffing
skewers
kitchen string
shallow roasting pan
wire rack

For the Madeira sauce:
Pour off all but 2 tablespoons fat from the roasting pan. Set the pan over moderate heat. Add the flour. Cook, stirring, for 3 minutes. Pour in the stock and simmer, stirring, until thickened. Add the lemon juice and Madeira, cover and cook for 2 minutes. Spoon some sauce over the duck. Serve the remaining sauce in a heated sauceboat.

1½ tablespoons flour
1¼ cups duck or chicken stock
juice of ½ lemon
1 cup Madeira wine

## Roast Potatoes

Peel the potatoes and cut in half lengthwise. Place on the rack of the roasting pan along with the duck during the last 45 minutes of roasting time.

3 red potatoes
3 sweet potatoes

## Cauliflower and Green Peas

4 quarts water
2 tablespoons salt
1 head cauliflower, cut into
flowerets
2 tablespoons butter

Bring water to a rapid boil in a large kettle. Add salt. Drop the flowerets into the water, and bring to a boil again. Boil slowly, uncovered, for 9 to 12 minutes. Cauliflower should be tender, but retain a suggestion of crunchiness. Remove the flowerets with a slotted spoon and place in a colander. Let the moisture evaporate for a moment. Arrange the flowerets around the circumference of a heated vegetable dish. Dot with the butter.

2 quarts water
1 tablespoon salt
2 cups peas, fresh or frozen

Bring salted water to a rapid boil in a large kettle. Add the peas and cook slowly, uncovered, for 4 to 8 minutes, until just tender. Drain the peas in a colander.

1 teaspoon sugar
salt and pepper to taste
2 tablespoons butter, cut into
pieces

Place the peas in a saucepan immediately after draining. Sprinkle in the sugar, salt and pepper. Roll the peas gently around over moderate heat for a few minutes to evaporate the moisture. Pour into the center of the heated vegetable dish.

## Raisin and Almond Mazurka

8 x 10-inch cake pan
shortening
2 tablespoons flour

Grease the bottom and sides of the cake pan with the shortening. Dust with the flour, coating the bottom and sides evenly. Set aside.

1 orange
1 lemon

Remove the outermost, orange-colored skin from the orange with a vegetable peeler. Do the same with the lemon. (The white part on the inside is bitter.) Drop the peelings into the saucepan and cover with cold water. Bring to a rapid boil and simmer for 2 minutes. Drain in a colander under cold running water for 1 minute. Pat the peels dry and cut into ⅛-inch strips.

¾ cup sugar
2 eggs
1¾ cups all-purpose flour
½ cup butter, melted
1 cup seedless raisins, chopped
½ cup almonds, blanched and
chopped
the orange and lemon peel

Combine the sugar and eggs in a large bowl. With an electric mixer, beat the mixture 2 to 3 minutes until it is pale. Sprinkle in ½ cup of the flour. Continue to beat while pouring in half of the melted butter. Sprinkle in another ½ cup of the flour and pour in the remaining butter, beating all the while, until the mixture is blended and smooth. Sprinkle in the chopped raisins. Sprinkle ¼ cup of flour over the raisins. With a rubber spatula, fold the mixture together. Sprinkle in the almonds, ¼ cup of the flour and fold together again. Sprinkle in the orange and lemon peel. Sprinkle in the remaining flour and fold together to blend thoroughly.

Press the dough mixture evenly into the cake pan. Bake in the middle level of a preheated 350° oven for 30 minutes. Cool on a wire rack for 5 minutes before serving.

Caviar-Stuffed Eggs with Garnishes,
Eggplant Zakuski with Buttered Black Bread

*Winter Melon Soup*
*Cold Sweet and Sour Vegetables*
*Prawns with Sweet Peppers*
*Spiced Lamb    Fried Rice*
*Eight=Precious Pudding*

### Winter Melon Soup

**9 small dried Chinese mushrooms**
**½ cup warm water**

Place the mushrooms in a small bowl; cover with the warm water. Soak for 30 minutes. Drain. Trim the stems of the mushrooms. Set aside.

**1½ pounds winter melon**

Peel the melon. Discard the inner seeds and stringy fibers. Cut the pulp into ¼-inch slices; cut the slices into 1½-inch pieces.

**1 ⅛-inch thick slice cooked ham**

Cut the ham into 1½-inch pieces and set aside.

**4½ cups chicken broth**
**the trimmed mushrooms**
**the melon pieces**
**the ham pieces**

Combine the chicken broth, mushrooms and melon in a heavy saucepan. Bring to a rapid boil. Reduce heat to low, cover and simmer for 15 minutes. Remove from heat and stir in the ham. Ladle the soup into a tureen and serve.

### Cold Sweet and Sour Vegetables

**1½ teaspoons salt**
**¼ cup soya sauce**
**2 tablespoons wine vinegar**
**2½ tablespoons brown sugar**
**1½ tablespoons sesame oil**

For the soya sauce mixture:
Combine the salt, soya sauce, wine vinegar, brown sugar and sesame oil in a small glass jar. Cover and shake until the sugar is dissolved. Use as needed for the vegetables.

**1 large cucumber**
**2 tablespoons soya sauce mixture**

Peel the cucumber. Dice into ¼-inch pieces. Place in a small serving bowl and add the soya sauce mixture. Stir to coat the cucumber. Chill well before serving.

**6 ribs celery**
**3½ tablespoons soya sauce mixture**

Wash the celery under cold water. Cut the celery into 1-inch slices. Place in a saucepan and cover with water. Bring to a rapid boil. Immediately drain in a colander and rinse under cold water for 1 minute. Drain. Place the celery slices in a small serving bowl and add the soya sauce mixture. Stir to coat the slices. Chill well before serving.

**2 bunches small radishes**
**4½ tablespoons soya sauce mixture**

Trim, wash and drain the radishes. Smash each radish slightly with the flat handle of a heavy knife, but leave the radish whole. Place the radishes in a small serving bowl and add the soya sauce mixture. Stir to coat the radishes. Chill well before serving.

### Prawns with Sweet Peppers

**3 sweet red peppers**
**¼ pound fresh mushrooms**
**¼ pound fresh broccoli**

Wash and core the peppers. Cut the peppers into rings. Set aside. Wash the mushrooms quickly under cold water and wipe clean. Trim off the stems. Wash the broccoli under cold water. Cut off the tough bottom stalks. Trim

*China*

the broccoli into 1½-inch pieces. Blanch the broccoli in 2 quarts boiling salted water for 5 minutes. Drain in a colander and rinse under cold running water. Drain on paper towels.

Heat the oil in a wok over moderately high heat. Add the sweet peppers and mushrooms and stir for 1 minute. Add the water, cover and simmer for 5 minutes. Remove with a slotted spoon and keep warm.

2 tablespoons oil
the peppers
the mushrooms
2 tablespoons water

Combine the prawns and broccoli in the wok. Sprinkle on the chopped onion and salt. Stir-fry for 2 to 3 minutes. Add the soya sauce, brown sugar, sherry and cucumber. Cook for 1 minute.

1 pound prawns, or shrimp, shelled and deveined
the broccoli
2 spring onions, chopped
½ teaspoon salt
2 tablespoons soya sauce
2 teaspoons brown sugar
2 tablespoons sherry
2-inch piece of cucumber, peeled and diced
2 teaspoons cornstarch
½ cup water

Mix the cornstarch with the water to a smooth paste. Lower the heat and add to the wok, stirring, until slightly thickened. Return the peppers and mushrooms to the pan and mix well. Serve immediately.

## Spiced Lamb

Wipe the meat and rub the salt into the skin. Place in a saucepan. Cover with water. Bring to a rapid boil. Reduce heat to a low simmer. Skim any froth that rises to the surface. Simmer the lamb, covered, for 20 minutes. Drain and set aside.

1 4-pound lamb leg or shoulder
1¼ teaspoons salt

Mix the soya sauce and sherry together in a small bowl. Crush the garlic and shred the ginger into the bowl. Blend together and rub into the lamb. Let stand for 10 minutes.

1½ tablespoons soya sauce
1½ tablespoons sherry
3 cloves garlic
1½ ounces green ginger or 1 teaspoon ground ginger

Heat the oil in a Dutch oven. Add the lamb and brown on all sides for 15 minutes. Pour on the beef bouillon. Bring to a rapid boil. Reduce heat to a simmer, cover and cook for 2½ hours.

5 tablespoons peanut oil
6 cups beef bouillon

Mix the cornstarch and water to a smooth paste in a small bowl. Lift the lamb onto a heated serving platter. Cover loosely and keep warm. Add the cornstarch mixture to the liquid in the pan. Bring to a boil, stirring constantly, until thickened. Pour the sauce over the lamb. Garnish with watercress.

1½ teaspoons cornstarch
1½ tablespoons cold water
watercress leaves

## Fried Rice

Pour the rice into a bowl. Cover with cold water. Stir the rice and water around with your hand. Drain. Repeat the washing process and drain again.

1½ cups long grain white rice

Place the rice in a saucepan with a tight-fitting lid. Measure in the water. Bring to a rapid boil, uncovered, over high heat. Boil for 2 to 3 minutes until holes appear in the surface of the rice. Cover the pan tightly and reduce heat to low. Cook the rice for 20 minutes. Turn off the heat but do not remove the lid. Let stand for 10 minutes. Remove the lid and fluff the rice with a fork.

the washed rice
3 cups cold water

salt and pepper to taste
2 tablespoons oil or lard
the cooked rice
2 eggs, lightly beaten

Season the rice with salt and pepper. Heat the oil or lard in a skillet or wok. Add the rice. Fry gently over medium heat for 10 minutes or until all the fat has been absorbed. Lower the heat. Pour the eggs onto the rice in a thin stream, stirring constantly. Continue to stir until the egg is mixed with the rice and just set. Serve immediately.

## Eight-Precious Pudding

1½ cups glutinous rice
(sweet rice)
1½ cups water

Cover the rice with cold water. Soak for 1 hour. Drain. Add the rice to 1½ cups water; bring to a simmer. Simmer for 15 minutes. Drain.

2 tablespoons lard
3 tablespoons sugar

Add lard and sugar. Stir to mix.

20 red dates
⅓ cup peanuts
⅓ cup walnut halves
¼ cup white seedless raisins
½ cup raisins
½ cup red and green candied cherries
¼ cup candied orange or lemon peel, cut into small pieces

Oil a 6-inch mold or heat-proof bowl. Decoratively arrange the fruits and nuts on the bottom and sides of the bowl. (They will cling to the sides.) Carefully place half of the rice in the bowl, covering the fruits and nuts.

½ cup canned sweet red bean paste

Spoon the red bean paste on the rice. Spoon on the remaining rice, gently packing it. Place the bowl in a steamer or on a rack in a wok. Steam the pudding for 1¼ hours.

¾ cup water
3 tablespoons sugar
1 tablespoon cornstarch, mixed with 2 tablespoons cold water
½ teaspoon vanilla

For the syrup:
Combine water and sugar in a small saucepan. Bring to a boil. Reduce heat to a simmer. Add cornstarch mixture; stir over low heat until thickened and clear. Stir in vanilla. Unmold pudding onto a serving plate. Spoon the syrup over the pudding. Serve hot.

*Clear Soup with Tofu and Shrimp*
*Crab Meat with Vinegar Dressing*
*Glazed Chicken Wings*
*Sukiyaki*
*Peas and Rice*
*Fresh Fruit in Pineapple Halves*

## Clear Soup with Tofu and Shrimp

**2 cups cold water**
**6 ounces tofu (soybean curd), cut into 6 cubes**
**1 2-inch square kombu (dried kelp), washed**

Bring the water to a simmer in a small saucepan. Add the tofu and kombu. Return to a simmer and immediately remove from the heat. Set aside until ready to serve.
Note: Tofu and Kombu may be obtained at Oriental specialty stores or larger supermarkets.

**2 cups salted water**
**6 spinach leaves**

Bring the salted water to a boil in another saucepan. Add the spinach. Return to a boil. Remove the spinach with a slotted spoon. Rinse under cold water. Squeeze the leaves to remove excess water and dry on a towel. Reserve the pan of cooking water.

**the reserved spinach water**
**6 medium-sized shrimp, shelled and deveined**

Return the reserved spinach water to a boil over high heat. Add the shrimp and boil for 30 seconds. Drain in a sieve and set aside.

**1½ quarts water**
**1 2-inch square kombu (dried kelp)**
**⅔ cup preflaked katsuobushi (dried bonito)**

For the stock:
Pour the water into a saucepan. Bring to a boil. Drop the kombu into the water. Return to a boil. Remove the kombu from the pan immediately with a slotted spoon and set aside. Stir the katsuobushi into the boiling water and remove from the heat. Let the stock rest for 2 minutes until the katsuobushi sinks to the bottom of the pan. With a large spoon, skim any froth that rises to the surface. Place a double thickness of cheesecloth in a sieve and set over a large bowl. Pour in the stock and drain slowly. Remove the katsuobushi and set aside.

**1½ teaspoons salt**
**½ teaspoon Japanese soy sauce**
**1 teaspoon sake**

Return the stock to the saucepan. Bring to a simmer over moderate heat. Stir in the salt, soy sauce, and sake.
Note: Reserve 2½ tablespoons of the stock for the following recipe.

**the spinach leaves**
**the tofu cubes**
**the shrimp**
**6 thin strips lemon peel**
**6 soup bowls**
**the soup stock**

Arrange a spinach leaf, a cube of tofu, 1 shrimp and a strip of lemon peel in the bottom of each bowl. Carefully fill each bowl ¾ full with the simmering stock. Serve immediately.

## Crab Meat with Vinegar Dressing

**1 large cucumber**
**½ cup cold water**
**1 teaspoon salt**

Peel the cucumber lengthwise in a striped pattern, cutting away and leaving alternate ¼-inch strips of peel. Halve lengthwise. Scoop out the seeds with a small spoon. Cut the halves crosswise into paper-thin slices. Combine the water and salt in a small bowl. Add the slices; soak for 30 minutes at room temperature. Drain, squeezing the slices to extract excess water.

| | 12 ounces fresh or canned crab meat |

Flake the crab meat and discard any cartilage or bone. Shred the meat with a large, sharp knife.

Equally divide the cucumber and crab meat into 6 small serving bowls. Wrap the ginger in a piece of cheesecloth and squeeze juice into each bowl. Serve with the dipping sauce.

the cucumber slices
the crab meat
3 tablespoons coarsely grated fresh gingerroot

For the dipping sauce:
Combine the rice vinegar, stock, sugar, soy sauce and salt in the small saucepan. Bring the sauce to a boil over high heat, stirring constantly. Immediately remove from heat and set aside. Cool to room temperature. Serve the dipping sauce in 6 tiny cups or dishes.

2½ tablespoons rice vinegar
2½ tablespoons fish stock, from preceding recipe or bottled clam juice
4 teaspoons sugar
2 teaspoons Japanese soy sauce
⅛ teaspoon salt

## Glazed Chicken Wings with Teriyaki Sauce

Lightly salt the chicken wings on both sides. Arrange the wings in a shallow baking pan. Place under a preheated broiler for 4 minutes. Turn over and broil 4 minutes.

18 meaty chicken wings
¾ teaspoon salt

For the sauce:
Combine the soy sauce, mirin and sugar in a small saucepan. Stir until heated through and sugar is dissolved. Cook the sauce for 2 minutes until thickened.

⅓ cup Japanese soy sauce
⅓ cup mirin (syrupy rice wine)
2 tablespoons sugar

Remove the wings from the broiler. Dip the wings into the sauce and drain. Return the wings to the broiler and broil for 4 minutes. Remove and dip into the sauce once more. Broil 2 to 3 minutes.

the broiled chicken wings

## Sukiyaki

Freeze the beef for 30 minutes to stiffen it slightly. Cut against the grain into ⅛-inch slices with a sharp, heavy knife. Cut the slices in half lengthwise.

1½ pounds beef sirloin

Bring the water to a boil. Drop in the shirataki and return to a boil. Drain and cut into thirds. Scrape the base of the bamboo shoot; slice in half lengthwise and cut the slices crosswise. Rinse under cold water and drain. Leave 3 inches of stem on the scallions. Cut into 1½-inch pieces. Peel the onion and cut into ½-inch slices. Wash the mushrooms and cut into ¼-inch slices.

1 8-ounce can shirataki (long thread-like noodles), drained
1 cup water
1 canned bamboo shoot
6 scallions
1 yellow onion
¼ pound fresh mushrooms

Arrange the meat, shirataki, bamboo shoot, scallion, onion, mushrooms, tofu and watercress attractively in separate rows on a large platter.

Use an electric skillet preheated to 425°, or heat a heavy skillet on a table-top cooking unit at the dining table.

the sliced beef
the shirataki
the sliced bamboo shoot
the scallion pieces
the sliced onion
the sliced mushrooms
2 cakes tofu, cut into 1-inch cubes
2 ounces watercress

Hold the beef suet with chopsticks and rub it over the bottom of the hot skillet. Add 6 to 8 slices of meat. Pour in ¼ cup soy sauce. Sprinkle the meat with the sugar. Cook for 1 minute, stirring. Turn the beef and push to one side of the skillet. Add ⅓ of the shirataki, bamboo shoot, scallions, onion, mushrooms, tofu and watercress. Sprinkle with ¼ cup rice wine. Lower the heat and maintain a steady simmer for 4 to 5 minutes. Transfer the meat and vegetables to individual serving plates with chopsticks and serve. Continue cooking in the same manner. If the skillet becomes too hot, lower heat and cool with a few drops of cold water.

1 large piece beef suet
¼ to ¾ cup Japanese soy sauce
3 tablespoons sugar
¾ cup rice wine

## Peas and Rice

Drop the peas into the boiling water. Cook for 1 minute. Drain in a colander and rinse under cold water. Drain again and set aside.

1 cup shelled fresh peas
2 quarts boiling salted water

Place the rice in a large bowl. Cover with cold water. Stir the rice and water around the bowl with your hand. Drain in a fine sieve. Repeat the process twice to remove any starchy powder. Drain thoroughly.

1½ cups short grain rice

Place the rice in a medium-sized saucepan with a tight fitting lid. Add the water and let stand for 10 minutes. Add the mirin and stir. Place the covered saucepan over high heat. Cook for 4 to 5 minutes. Reduce to medium heat and cook for 8 to 10 minutes.

the washed rice
1¾ cups water
1½ tablespoons mirin (syrupy rice wine)

Add the peas to the rice, cover and cook over high heat for 20 to 30 seconds. This will help dry the rice. Remove from the heat. Let the cooked rice steam itself, covered, for 10 to 15 minutes.

the blanched peas

Gently toss the rice and peas. Scoop out individual portions. Sprinkle the sesame seed and salt mixture over each portion. Serve immediately.

1½ tablespoons mixture black sesame seeds and coarse salt

## Fresh Fruit in Pineapple Halves

Hull and wash the strawberries. Halve the cantaloupe. Scoop the flesh into balls with a melon-ball cutter. Halve the pineapple lengthwise keeping the leaves in place. Cut out the core, remove flesh and cut into 1-inch pieces. Fill the pineapple halves with the fruit and serve.

1 pint fresh strawberries
1 cantaloupe
1 pineapple

Clear Soup with Tofu and Shrimp

## Christmas Day
## Menu for Six

Cranberry-Orange Relish
Poached Pear Halves
Ham Baked in Pastry Crust
Raisin Sauce
Curried Corn Timbale
Cheesecake with Raspberry Sauce

### Pear Halves Filled with Cranberry-Orange Relish

For the relish:
Combine the cranberries and water in a saucepan. Bring to a simmer. Cook slowly just until the cranberry skins pop. Remove from heat and stir for a moment. Set aside.

Peel the outermost, orange-colored part of the orange skin with a vegetable peeler. Reserving the fruit, place the peelings in a saucepan and cover with water. Bring water to a simmer for 2 minutes. Drain in a colander under cold running water. Return the peel to the saucepan and repeat the process, simmering for 2 minutes. Remove from heat and drain in a colander under cold running water. Cut the peel into strips 1/16 inch wide. Add to the cranberries.

Completely peel the oranges, removing as much of the membrane as possible. Separate the oranges into sections and chop into small pieces. Add to the cranberries. Add the brown sugar and cinnamon, stirring until well blended. Taste the cranberries. If too tart, add more sugar. Refrigerate until chilled.

For the poached pears:
Combine the sugar and water in a saucepan. Bring to a simmer, stirring until the sugar is dissolved. Add the lemon juice. Simmer for 5 minutes. Cover and set aside.

Add the lemon juice to the bowl of cold water. Peel, halve and core the pears; drop into the bowl of cold water with lemon juice.

Return the syrup to a simmer. Add 4 pear halves to the syrup. Simmer for 8 minutes until the pears are tender. Remove the pears with a slotted spoon and put in a bowl. Poach the remaining pears in the same manner. Pour the syrup over the pears and chill until ready to use. Before serving, drain the pear halves on a wire rack. Fill the centers with the cranberry-orange relish. Arrange the pear halves around the ham.

### Ham Baked in Pastry Crust

Remove the rind from the ham. Cut off all but ⅛ inch of the fat from the ham with a sharp knife.

**Ingredients (left column):**

1 16-ounce package of fresh cranberries
½ cup cold water

1 medium, bright-skinned orange

1 medium orange
the peeled orange
⅓ cup firmly packed brown sugar
pinch cinnamon

½ cup sugar
1½ cups water
¼ cup lemon juice

juice of ½ lemon
a bowl of cold water
6 firm ripe pears

12-pound boneless, smoked ham

Set the ham in a deep roasting pan. Combine the wine, raisins and sugar in a small saucepan. Bring to a simmer. Remove from the heat and let stand 10 minutes. Pour the mixture over the ham. Roast, uncovered, in a preheated 350° oven for 2½ hours, basting frequently.

1 cup red Burgundy wine
½ cup raisins
1 tablespoon sugar

For the pastry:
Combine the flour, baking powder, salt, mustard and sage in a large bowl. Stir with a fork to blend thoroughly.

6 cups sifted all-purpose flour
4 teaspoons baking powder
1¾ teaspoons salt
¾ teaspoon powdered mustard
¼ teaspoon powdered sage
½ cup cold butter, cut into pieces
½ cup shortening, chilled
1½ cups cold milk

Drop the butter into the flour mixture a few pieces at a time and cover with the flour. Cut chilled shortening into the flour with a pastry blender until the mixture resembles coarse meal. Gradually add the cold milk to make a soft, but not sticky, dough. Place the dough on a lightly floured board. Knead for 1 minute, shaping into a smooth ball. Wrap in a sheet of waxed paper and refrigerate.

When the ham has finished roasting, carve into serving slices. Assemble the slices into original shape of the ham.

Mix the honey with the wine basting sauce. Using a pastry brush, coat the ham with the mixture.

3 tablespoons honey
3 tablespoons wine basting sauce
cold milk

Roll out the refrigerated dough in a sheet ¼ inch thick. Fold over the ham, covering it completely. Make a hole in the top of the dough to allow steam to escape during baking. Place the ham on a large, lightly buttered baking sheet. Make cut-out Christmas designs with the leftover dough. Place on the dough covering the ham. Bake in a preheated 450° oven for 15 minutes. Lower the heat to 350° and bake the ham 45 minutes. Brush the crust twice with cold milk during the baking time. The crust will turn a delicate brown. Let the ham stand at room temperature for 15 minutes before serving.

## Raisin Sauce

Spoon off fat from the wine basting liquid. Strain through a sieve into a saucepan. Discard the basting raisins. Add the ¾ cup fresh raisins and sugar to the pan. Simmer for 2 minutes. Add the brown sauce. Serve in a warmed sauceboat with the ham.

¾ cup wine basting liquid from the cooked ham
¾ cup seedless raisins
1½ tablespoons brown sugar
1 cup brown sauce

For the brown sauce:
Melt the butter in a heavy saucepan. Add the chopped vegetables. Sauté, stirring occasionally, until they just begin to turn golden.

2 tablespoons butter
¼ cup chopped carrot
¼ cup chopped onion
¼ cup chopped celery

Stir in the flour. Cook the vegetables, stirring constantly, until they are a rich brown color. Remove the pan from the heat. Stir in the beef stock, using a wire whisk to blend smoothly. Add the parsley, bay leaf, garlic and thyme to the sauce. Continue to cook, stirring the mixture frequently, until it thickens.

2 tablespoons flour
1 cup beef stock, heated
1 sprig parsley
⅓ bay leaf
½ clove garlic, crushed
pinch thyme

Add the beef stock and tomato paste. Simmer slowly for 1 hour. The sauce should reduce to 1 cup. Skim off any fat that has accumulated on the surface. The sauce is ready to use or may be refrigerated overnight.

1 cup beef stock, heated
1 teaspoon tomato paste

## Curried Corn Timbale

Beat the eggs until well blended in a large bowl. Add the corn and the creamed corn. Stir in the Swiss cheese, Cheddar cheese, cream, bread crumbs, minced onion, parsley, curry powder, salt and pepper.

Butter the bottom and sides of the 8-cup mold. Line the bottom with waxed paper cut to size and shape. Pour the mixture into the mold. Set in a baking dish filled with boiling water ⅔ the way up the side of the mold. Place the dish on the lower-middle level of a preheated 350° oven and bake 30 minutes. Reduce the heat to 325° and bake 45 to 60 minutes. Be sure the water surrounding the mold never reaches a simmer. The timbale is done when it has risen to the top of the mold and cracked open on top. Keep the timbale in the turned-off oven, with the door open, for 10 minutes before unmolding. Place a plate upside down over the top of the mold and turn the timbale onto the plate.

6 eggs
1½ cups fresh or frozen corn
1 12-ounce can creamed corn
⅓ cup grated Swiss cheese
⅓ cup grated Cheddar cheese
⅔ cup heavy cream
⅔ cup fresh bread crumbs
3 tablespoons minced onion
¼ cup chopped fresh parsley
½ teaspoon curry powder
1 teaspoon salt
¼ teaspoon pepper

an 8-cup timbale or charlotte mold or soufflé dish
softened butter
waxed paper

## Cheesecake with Raspberry Sauce

Blend the crumbs and sugar in a bowl. Pour in the butter. Stir with a fork to moisten the mixture. Grease a 9-inch springform pan with softened butter. Using a soup spoon, press the crumbs firmly onto the bottom and sides of the pan.

1½ cups graham cracker crumbs
1 tablespoon brown sugar
¼ cup butter, melted
1 tablespoon butter, softened

For the filling:
Place the cream cheese in a large mixing bowl to soften. Or you may soften the cream cheese more quickly if you spread it around the bowl with a fork. Blend in the vanilla, flour, sugar and salt. Beat with an electric mixer until fluffy. Add the egg yolks and beat thoroughly. Beat in the lemon juice and heavy cream.

1 pound cream cheese
1 teaspoon vanilla
¼ cup all-purpose flour
2 tablespoons sugar
¼ teaspoon salt
4 egg yolks, lightly beaten
1 tablespoon lemon juice
1 cup heavy cream

Beat the egg whites in another bowl until soft peaks form. Gradually beat in the sugar until the meringue is stiff and glossy. Fold the meringue into the cream cheese mixture. Pour the mixture into the pan. Bake in a preheated 325° oven for 1½ hours until set in the center. Turn off the oven, leave the door ajar and let the cake cool in the oven. Chill the cake until firm before removing from the pan.

4 egg whites
2 tablespoons sugar

For the raspberry sauce:
Heat the jelly in a medium-sized saucepan. Add the raspberries and simmer for a moment. Stir in the lemon juice. Remove from heat and force through a fine sieve. Chill and serve with the cheesecake.

1 cup currant jelly
1 quart raspberries
2 tablespoons lemon juice

Ham Baked in Pastry Crust, Poached Pears
Filled with Cranberry-Orange Relish, Raisin Sauce

Index

64

***Christmas Around the World*** is a collection of traditional holiday dishes as varied as the people who have developed them. The menus in this cookbook are representative of the numerous traditional meals served in countries around the world, including such time-honored dishes as:

- Roast Prime Rib and Plum Pudding from England
- Rice and Almond Pudding from Denmark
- Buche de Noel from France
- Fruitcake Panettone from Italy

Sample the foods from *Christmas Around the World* and experience a delightful journey around the world without ever leaving home. *Bon Appetit!*

0-8249-3008-8 295